"Only once in a lifetime do we come across a writer like Danté Stewart, so young and yet so masterful with the pen. This work, this *Shoutin' in the Fire,* is a thing to make dungeons shake and hearts thunder. Each line is packed with such glowing wisdom and grounding love that it makes the eyes tear and the hair raise on the backs of necks. It has the lyrical prowess of a good sermon, yes, but the rhythm is entirely ancestral, like it was conveyed by our departed elders from their intimate prayer circles. What is most striking is Stewart's commitment to truth-telling in the Black Christian liberation tradition, which is indeed remarkable given how others who refer to themselves as such eschew truth for the warm embrace of dogma. That, in itself, is what makes *Shoutin' in the Fire* tongue-speak, hosanna, holy, the kind of clarion call that would make Maya Angelou hoot and James Baldwin holler."

—Robert Jones, Jr., *New York Times* bestselling author of *The Prophets*

"Danté Stewart has given us a generational gift. With compelling storytelling, beautiful writing, and incisive, prophetic insight, he gives us a vision of a world that longs to burst forth if we had ears to hear."

—Rich Villodas, lead pastor of New Life Fellowship and author of *The Deeply Formed Life*

"Extraordinary . . . a moving wake-up call to us all."

—Katherine Stewart, author of *The Power Worshippers*

SHOUTIN'
IN THE FIRE

An American Epistle

DANTÉ STEWART

CONVERGENT
NEW YORK

Published in the United States by Convergent Books,
an imprint of Random House, a division of Penguin
Random House LLC, New York.

CONVERGENT BOOKS is a registered trademark and its C colophon
is a trademark of Penguin Random House LLC.

Library of Congress Cataloging-in-Publication Data
Names: Stewart, Danté, author.
Title: Shoutin' in the fire / Danté Stewart.
Description: New York: Convergent, 2021.
Identifiers: LCCN 2021024076 (print) |
LCCN 2021024077 (ebook) |
ISBN 9780593239629 (hardcover) | ISBN 9780593239636 (ebook)
Subjects: LCSH: Stewart, Danté. | African Americans—
Religion. | Christian biography—Georgia—Augusta.
Classification: LCC BR1725.S7449 A3 2021 (print) |
LCC BR1725.S7449 (ebook) | DDC 270.092 [B]—dc23
LC record available at https://lccn.loc.gov/20210240762

PRINTED IN THE UNITED STATES OF AMERICA ON ACID-FREE PAPER

crownpublishing.com

2 4 6 8 9 7 5 3 1

First Edition

For
Jasamine, Asa, Ava,
and all who dream of
love and liberation

Here you were to be loved. To be loved, baby, hard at once and forever to strengthen you against the loveless world.

—JAMES BALDWIN, "MY DUNGEON SHOOK"

CONTENTS

Introduction: The Fire   3

Wages.   11

Terror.   41

Rage.   78

Back Roads.   99

Wound.   132

Flooding.   169

Pieces.   203

American.   223

Breath.   243

Acknowledgments   255

SHOUTIN' IN THE FIRE

INTRODUCTION

THE FIRE

There's an old King James Version Bible sitting on my bookshelf. It is black, rugged; the gold lining on the pages shines as light hits it. The jacket is missing, and the threads have unloosened from one another over the years. It has been tried. It has traveled across the South, across time. Now it sits on a shelf where it keeps the company of books written by Black folk. Black folk who have read a similar Bible, who have wrestled with it, been confused by it. Black folk who have held it as tight as I do today.

When I open up this old Bible, dusty words emerge, conjuring up memories of poetic sermons and sweaty mics smelling like old metal and stank breath. I am suddenly surrounded by preachers and mothers and friends and saints and sinners who tried to love and live well—while failing, learning, and trying again. When I read these ancient scriptures, I hear the way they flowed from my momma's lips. What was it about this book that kept her up in the middle of the night, calling on the Lord, calling out our names, calling out things that she imagined possible for all of us? What was it that kept her crying out when the world around her was burning?

When she recited scripture, she spoke it poetically, adding the old *eth* at the end of words like the King James Version did. Those words carried the divine. It was as transporting as fiction, yet nothing like fiction. Something you could only call magical, yet nothing like magic. The words were an entire world, but they were also in her Black body in this white country. These words carried both weight and worth and worship and worry and whatever "w" words you can describe—words that put you back together again when you, your body, and your country are shattered. It was honest, it was close, it flowed from her heart and her lips. This was her language. It was the language of my grandmother, the language of her mother, the language of all the Black folk between our yellow house, my grandma's red brick house, and the white-stained brick church that told us we were somebody. Indeed, to hear this language is to hear the voice of God upon us in a land that has never truly known God or Love or Blackness.

That is the interesting thing about living in America. And being Black. And doing both while being a

Christian. We are caught between a terrifying and inescapable reality: the Bible, the country, and the body.

So when my momma prayed this language, she was praying against the country that has been decided for us. She was praying against the same reality that she grew up caught in between. My momma learned this language in 1960s South Carolina, in a world anointed by the sermons of AME preachers, Black revolutionaries, and working-class and poor people. She took this language—borrowed from scripture and sermon alike—and used it to protect us, cover us. She made sure we'd learn this language, too—of prayer and hope, of resistance and creation.

When we were growing up, our house was full of these kinds of sermons: Black people singing songs over Sunday dinners. Arguing over the ways we have failed one another. Discussing Black books, and Black art, and Black schools, and Black love, and Black food, and old pictures of afros and bell-bottoms. It was all Black language—a way of taking back what was stolen from us, taking back the love that we lost, taking back our bodies from destruction. It is a language they at once inherited and created. It is a language we, too, inherit and still create and stretch and revive.

Even to this day, my mother still calls out those old, familiar words to me. I have taken them to be my own words. These words may never deliver us or shake the foundations of the country, but they've brought us this far.

And still today we continue, finding ways to create and name all that is meaningful and loving. We know that we will have to learn how to breathe through the suffocation, live through the terror, and find a way to take those old black Bibles, and those old Black books, and our tired Black hearts, and our weary Black feet, and be there for one another in ways Black folk have done before, and ways our Black mommas learned, and ways our Black daddies taught us.

I don't know if our country has taken time to look itself in the mirror to question the ways it keeps us up at night and makes it hard to pray. I wonder if the country I love can imagine itself as being better than the ways it has learned to be terrible. I fear that the same country that my momma had to live in is the same country my children and theirs will have to live in.

As I live and move and have my being in this country, I wonder to myself: *How do I be Black and Christian and American?*

So I return to this old King James Bible, and our Black prayers, and Black sermons, and Black songs, and Black poems, and all the ways Black folk have learned how to live in a country that does not love us. I return because I have so much more to learn about love—and how to love in ways that are honest, and brutal, and beautiful. I return because there is something to be said to me. I don't go to that old Bible and our Black books and words to convince myself that the terrible things will eventually get better. No. I return because I know that there is something about these words that the old Black country folk held on to in the burning.

One morning last August, my body felt heavy as I slowly made my way downstairs to make my coffee. We had somehow endured yet another summer of violence—this time just with more of the world's attention. The sun crept through our windows; my son was sleeping soundly, and my wife was asleep upstairs. I was struck at how ordinary this moment was—the house was still, quiet—yet chaos ravaged my mind, my body, all the way down to my feet. A gnawing rage and sadness sat trapped in my body. I didn't want to feel anything. But I knew I must feel everything.

I needed a way to think about all of the hell that was happening in our country. Numbers that kept climbing. Public lynchings. Hashtags. Eulogies. So I sat at our wooden table and cracked open my dusty Bible to join the cloud of witnesses. To see the ways they held their crosses, feeling every splinter—and to see the ways they were led at night by fire. As I sat and sipped, I listened.

As I read the Hebrew Bible, I am struck by two main verbs that refer to waiting. One is to wait with expectation; the other is to wait in the tension of enduring. It is not passive. It is an active struggle to live in the face of despair. I think of my mother, the ways in which she would conjure up Old Testament stories, making dead bones come alive, turning and twisting words like lyrics from love songs. She loved telling the story about the three Hebrew boys in the fire. The three boys, who endured unspeakable horrors, who had the audacity to live and dance and to shake off the chains, was not just a good story. Their bodies, their struggle, and their surviving was my momma's own.

When I think about my momma and how much she and all those Black folk held on to old stories, I don't just see people who courageously shook kingdoms and who preach audacious messages of liberation. I also see people who know what it means to live with deep trauma and still love themselves enough to believe in their future. I see them like the prophets, trying to shake kingdoms and rock souls and straighten bodies back up again and love us in simple ways that cooled our bodies and cooled our spirits and stopped our trembling.

To believe in the better, to believe in your future, to shout in the midst of a country on fire, to stare down lions, to shake the foundations of the empire, to make meaning in the face of death, to fail, to create, to live, and to love—this is the stuff of hope. It is not an assent to nostalgia or myths or lies. It is the audacious belief that one's body, one's story, one's future does not end in this moment.

The three Hebrew boys that my momma loved to talk about underwent two fires: a physical burning in a furnace, and a prolonged burning set ablaze by empire. These boys didn't simply make it through the fires, somehow just embracing the violence of the empire politely and passively. The miracle was their audacity. The miracle was their courage to stare down terror. The miracle was the revelation that violent empires don't have the last say. Empires may be able to enslave our people, plunder our resources; they may try to destroy both our bodies and our future. But in the midst of the burning, we somehow try to liberate ourselves, again and again, showing something more deep, more honest, and more powerful than the blazing. Empires will not always win. Empires will not always win.

In Audre Lorde's "A Litany of Survival," she writes: "So it is better to speak / remembering / we were never meant to survive."

I am both shocked and terrified that my momma and I have survived, that we are a part of a people who have survived. I am terrified because it is a reminder, as Lorde writes, that "we were never meant to survive." It was intended that the beauty upon our bodies blessed of God and kissed by nature's sun would be destroyed.

"We were never meant to survive." It is both a lyric and a lesson.

The story I want to tell is this: Our lives are not just resistance. Our lives are not just lessons. We are not heroes. We are not villains. We are human—as beautiful as we are terrible.

And we are worthy of the deepest love.

WAGES.

Our humanity is our burden, our life; we
need not battle for it; we need only do
what is infinitely more difficult—that is, accept it.
—JAMES BALDWIN

"The truth shall set you free," my momma always told me. But it was lying that gave me
power.

The year is 1998. My name is "Debra's Boy" to
the Pentecostals, "Little Calvin" to my uncles. "Vac-
uum Boy," my daddy will call me jokingly from the
living room, before he adds, "It's time to clean up."
And to my momma: "Boy." She'll say, "Boy."

I am skinny. My feet are wide. Black Nike Air
Force 1s are my shoe of choice come time to pick
out the one pair of shoes we get a year. The white,
dusty South Carolina dirt sits in the cracks of the

swoosh. I wear my Carmelo Anthony jersey everywhere. White, red numbers, his name covering my
own. Most days I'm on a dirt court, shooting a ball
that is barely inflated. I'll dribble in the thick, swel-
tering South Carolina heat. Sometimes when I shoot,
I close my eyes and run into a future where I imagine
myself as Carmelo. A name remembered, called.

THE YEAR IS 2006. MY NAME IS "CHURCH BOY" TO MY
friends. They have heard that I had the Holy Ghost.
They have heard that me, my family, and all the Black
folk between my grandmother's red brick house and
our white-stained brick church speak in an unknown
language, and sweat like we are on fire, burning.

In the morning, on the bus, I scramble to finish
homework in my seat. We pass the Baptist church,
the gas station where we'd get our chicken and livers
and hot sauce, and my old elementary school that got
shut down, on our way to Calhoun County High
School.

I get off the bus and walk onto campus with my
busted black book bag revealing busted black books.
My hair is short, barely curly, barely brushed. I have
on an oversized white shirt like we would see in
music videos.

"What's up, Church Boy!" my friend Jakeem says
to me as I enter class.

I nod at him.

"Nigga," Jakeem says, "we gon' ball out or what?" We talk about all the yards I was going to get rushing. I am a running back who can never wait for Friday nights when the stadium lights are on and I think I am Reggie Bush. I think about all the ways Reggie ran, and all the ways I want to run.

"Nigga," I tell Jakeem, dapping him up, smiling, "now you know we gon' ball."

THE YEAR IS 2010. MY NAME IS "STEW." I AM BIGGER, older. I'm still Debra's son and Church Boy—but I am also beginning anew, or so I think.

I step onto Clemson University's campus where I'll be playing football for the next four years. The day is hot. South Carolina's furnace is unyielding, scorching. I barely know anyone. I barely know myself.

On this afternoon, we're preparing for the Big Weigh-In.

"Ayeeee, my dawg," another player says, as we walk into the weight room together. "Nigga," he says, in a joking voice, his Atlanta accent coming out, "whatdehell you got on?"

I look down at my brown loafers, no socks, feet smelling like burnt rubber and baking soda.

"What?" I say, imitating his slow Atlanta drawl. "Whatyoumean?" We dap each other up.

"Who you is?" he says.

"I'm Stew," I say. "Good to meet you, my nigga. What about you?"

"GP," he says. "You hear about all the running them boys did in the summer? They say we gonna do a lot of running in fall camp."

"Nah, nigga," I say, thinking about how much I feel the sun beat on my face already, my shirt sticking to my body like I just went swimming. "I ain't heard nothing about that!"

GP takes his hat off to wipe the sweat off his face and laughs. "Well, you better get ready."

I am barely in shape. I know I am fast, but I am not ready to work out like that.

"Boy gonna need some Gatorade and some AC," he says.

I laugh. "Nah, nigga, we gon' be straight."

I feel at home. I don't really know who I am. I've been struggling with all these names my whole young life, running into dreams wherever I can find them. But for now, at least, I am home.

CLEMSON WAS GREEN. YEAR-AROUND THE GRASS looked like someone spray-painted it. There are trees everywhere. Between the stadium and the classrooms that I would arrive to in my orange joggers and hoodie was nothing but hills. The winters are cold. Chilly. Dark. The summers are scorching, hot, sticky.

The springs are unbearable for my allergies. The falls are, as they say, God's country. There are tiger paws imprinted on the street leading up to the brick building bearing the name of a slaveholder; some are orange, some are white. We would make jokes that we were the *actual* university of South Carolina, though another school in the capital of the state bore the name.

If you travel the right way, you can see the Blue Ridge mountains, their hues a bit of gray, a bit of white, a bit of blue, in the background. It is an agriculture school, which means that you could travel any direction and pass country fields full of haystacks, and old gas stations that made you feel like you were in the fifties or sixties. That part felt like home.

Game days at Clemson were full of excitement. Everything would shut down. Traffic would make you feel like you were in Atlanta. Cars would creep slowly; there was hardly movement because of the sheer amount of people coming to see the Tigers play. Our buses would be led to town. The police cars' lights would be shining. The place would become still as we'd creep over the hill to arrive for the Tiger walk. It was like nothing I had seen before. Hundreds of people would greet us, their hands reaching out to touch us, trying to get us to sign their shirts, their footballs, their faces, sometimes even their children. At the end of every game, fans would storm the field just to sing the university's song. They would put their hands around our shoulders, sway side to side, as we lifted up our hands in salute to the paw that brought us both to the same place.

I loved every bit of it.

We were beloved. And why shouldn't we have been? We gave fans stories to talk about with their families around the dinner table. We had given them reason to brave the long hills. We had given them tears. We had given them meaning. And in the midst of it all we had given them something they never deserved: We gave them confidence that the football field was the world and that the world was okay and what mattered most between both of our lives was our ability to run fast, jump high, and give them more things to talk about with their families.

"Everybody has a place here," our coach would say. And I believed it. But not everybody had the home that we thought it would be.

MY FRESHMAN YEAR, I JOINED THE GOSPEL CHOIR ON campus. It became a way of feeling some type of connection to back home for many of us. Whether you were raised Methodist, Baptist, Pentecostal, or something in between, the gospel choir became a way for all the Black students on the white campus to connect with one another. Gospel choir was like the sanctuary where it wasn't weird or different or something foreign to hear praise breaks and testimonies and altos, sopranos, and tenors and white students and Black students singing into all times of the night.

That's where I met Jasamine, a beautiful Black girl from the Black rural South like me. She was charming, neither an extrovert nor wholly reserved. She was brown, her hair touching her eyes, and then her shoulders, and then the middle of her back. She could sing, so good, and so much lovelier than I played the drums. As we would rehearse, I used to catch eyes with her in between songs, in between me looking down at my phone and picking up the sticks to go through the next song. Her caramel-colored eyes made me forget about all the ways I had learned how to run.

She kept me coming back again and again. I loved Jesus, yes, and I loved drums, but I actually liked being around her as much as I loved both. A few months into gospel choir we started talking. Then we started seeing each other. Then we started dating. She not only became my girlfriend, but she was the only way I remained really connected to Black Clemson.

The old folk back home always gave me two pieces of dating advice when they knew I was going off to the white school: 1. Don't bring home no white girl. 2. Get you somebody who loves Jesus. I never gave that too much thought. I just know that when I met Jas and we started dating, I had made good on the lessons that they had taught me.

Around the same time, some *very nice white Christians,* as my grandma would call them, invited me and some of my teammates to their college fellowship. They were the type of nice that would make you feel warm inside. The kind you thought was good because they didn't really ask too much of you. They were the type of nice that made other Black people talk about how nice they were. Nice enough to make me curious.

When Thursday night rolled around, I decided to visit. The fellowship was held in the center of campus, in the largest auditorium inside the building. People were lining up outside to get in. You could already hear the music even before you stepped in the door. As soon as I walked in, everything about it said "You wanna be here." At least five hundred people. But there was no choir. There was no Kirk Franklin. There was no shouting. Just the dim lights, young white kids in khakis and polos, and older white kids in skinny jeans and washed shirts. It was kind of corny but it felt good. I was eighteen, and I loved the feeling of belonging in a place where everyone flocked to on Thursdays. You felt like you were at a concert or something. It was like our bodies were consumed, like we launched ourselves in it. You didn't have to do anything, either; you just showed up and enjoyed the show. I noticed I was one of the few Black people as far as I could see. I noticed everyone was treating me extra nice. It was so different from gospel choir, where maybe thirty of us met in a small room in the student center.

Soon, I felt my rural Black Pentecostal self intersecting with stories much different from my own. I met people who didn't eat liver and hot sauce like we would as kids. I met people who never heard of shouting in church, running through the woods with sticks, playing basketball on dirt courts, and getting yelled at for spray-painting the old trailers around the neighborhood. I met people and lived with people and sang with people who were not Black. I was introduced to white Catholics, evangelicals, atheists, progressives, conservatives. They, like me, were simply trying to make sense of their stories.

The thing I didn't realize was that both of our stories had already been told by this nation in ways that we would later have to reckon with. We were walking into scripts that had already been written. We were individuals but we were also performers. Later I would come to understand that my body and this lesson would have a haunting meeting. This story was told in ways that saw them as beautiful, innocent, worthy. Though I didn't know it at the time and would later learn this lesson in the most terrible ways, the story saw me and those who looked like me as less than. They were deserving of being at Clemson. *We* were the ones that simply should be grateful.

And so I was. Grateful. I soon learned that I was not like the other Black people; I was the exception. They wanted me there, I believed. To be told that I was not like other Black people felt like praise. It felt like belonging. But I didn't know to care, either: I was home. I had made it. I was the exception.

I STARTED GOING TO THE WHITE MEGACHURCH IN TOWN more. I became exceptional at running from the spirituals, long church nights, hot sweaty sermons, and all the things that made me who I was. I was finding the belonging and worth I'd ached for for so long—but it was coming at a price. The way I talked became unfamiliar to many of my friends back home.

I became exceptional at making white people comfortable, and, ignorant, I never really called into question why I in my exception was the only Blackness they encountered. I believed that the name on the back of my jersey, as clear as the numbers on the front, meant I was better and that distance from Blackness was like scoring touchdowns or getting interceptions: Each brought your name closer to the mouths of white people and further away from the lives of your people. It was a powerful appeal. It was the cost of "making" it in a white world that cared only about my body in performance or in pain. To win like white folk won, to be remembered, and to forget those who got you there, this was the price of the ticket.

It happened slowly, insidiously, but surely: I was running from home. Every time I would make a trip home, I could tell that my people were starting to see me differently. I remember talking about the music and how I had heard through a YouTube video that Black Pentecostals that looked like us and worshipped like us were not really "saved." That all the ways my people loved us didn't matter, or wasn't enough. My deeply formed Pentecostal practices and community life, my roots, were now planted in different soil.

For I believed that this is what it meant to be Christian: to hold a perspective that was objective, neutral, airtight, without error. Yet all the while up-holding the beliefs and systems that see Black mommas and Black daddies and Black children this way, but as less than, less valued, less smart. In my pursuit to be a better Christian, I didn't question any of it. I viewed Black sermons, and Black songs, and Black buildings with skepticism; and white sermons, and white songs, and white buildings with sacredness. I believed the lie.

So I kept listening to white sermons and white songs, for I had finally "made" it. I was somebody. I found white affirmation. I found white celebration. I found white protection. I lost myself. I lost the Black world I came from. The cost didn't matter. The rewards of whiteness were too great.

TRAYVON GOT MURDERED WHEN I WAS A SOPHOMORE. I remember other Black teammates on the football team around me were so shaken by the death of someone who looked like us. Some of my teammates lamented the reality of being Black and young and terrified, fearing they would never be protected in the world the ways we knew we were protected on the field.

I had learned the same lessons as a kid. My mother and father would make sure that we knew how fragile the balance our lives hung in. So they taught me and my sister and my brothers and all of the children at church to make sure that we always talked the right way, acted the right way, and never really made too much noise about what was happening in the world, lest what happened to them would happen to us.

I used this as an excuse to stay quiet. So I was a part of the group that didn't really want to rock the boat, lest I get on the bad side of the coaches, and become what they liked to call *a distraction*.

So I kept quiet.

Somewhere in my mind, I knew there was so much to hate about the world. And so much we needed to talk about. And so, so much to pray about.

But what mattered most was me making sure that my name and "trouble" stayed out of the same sentences. I was not a scholarship player. My place was not secure. I could not afford to be a distraction; I needed to be what they deemed *dependable*. I was just a walk-on trying to get some playing time. I was doing real good that year, too. I knew I was getting noticed more by the coaches, since I had just come off a good winter and had a good spring ball. When my teammates asked me to join them taking a photo in black hoodies in solidarity, I said "I got to go to study hall." That was a lie. I didn't have anything to do. I didn't care. That was their thing and I was doing my thing. In my mind: Yes, I was Black, but I was really a football player who just happened to be Black. More important than Trayvon's Black body being murdered and our Black bodies taking a photo was my Black body's distance from both. Being good at football was more important than being Black.

I had worked hard to become the best athlete and the best man I could be, as our coaches would always say. I had succeeded.

During spring ball my coach raved about how good I was doing, how much I was progressing as a leader, and how proud he was that I was accomplishing so much in a short amount of time. "Ma," I said as I called my momma one day on the way home from practice. "Coach mentioned me in the news conference." We were both so proud together that her baby was giving her something she could talk about on Sunday when she went to church.

One year earlier, I'd been just a walk-on trying to get some attention and earn my place on the team. Now, I'd finally made it happen.

But by the time the next year rolled around, my status was in jeopardy.

One of my teammates—let's call him DJ—was a top-rated cornerback who came in with other top recruits. He enrolled early in school before the rest of the freshmen athletes arrived in the fall. DJ was the kind of player even *upperclassmen* would talk about— barely in college, yet already a legend. For a walk-on like me, that wasn't good news.

That summer, I kept trying to suppress how afraid I was of losing my position on the team. I mean damn, I'd worked so hard for it. And I wasn't ready to admit that I was about to lose it. I was too scared to tell my momma. Too ashamed to tell my daddy. Too arrogant to tell myself.

I'd put my all into this role. And deep in my bones, I knew this young dude was about to come and take it from me.

So I began to run.

One day in the summer of that year, before we went out for practice, one of my coaches called me into the office and asked me what was going on. I knew what that meant. He was wondering why I wasn't working out the way that I should, why I wasn't really showing up. In my mind, I'm thinking, *How in the world Coach know this? Who told him?* I was pissed. I gave him some answers about how I was struggling with school or something. I knew how to maneuver my face and change my voice to make people feel bad for me. It wasn't my first time lying. I knew how to wear the mask. Coach nodded sympathetically and let me go.

Later that day, I went out to practice. It was my turn up at defensive back. I ran onto the field to take my place while the other players cleared out. But DJ stayed on the field. "I ain't moving," he said.

At first, I was ready to fight. Thinking *Who this dude think he is?* All summer I heard people talk about how good he was. So when he didn't move off the field, I knew he saw me as someone in *his* way. He still ain't moved. Some of our teammates felt the tension. They knew I wasn't really into conflict like that. Some of them called me "the Preacher," the way I posted Bible verses all the time on my social media, and led us in prayer from time to time. *Church Boy.* As pissed as I was, I felt the pressure of that name—and the anxiety of losing it. Maybe my teammates felt the need to protect that in me, too. So our teammates got in between us, separated us. DJ went on to play, and I stood on the sideline.

I immediately felt regret, resentful—both a rage and an anxiety. I had just lost my place, something coaches and teammates had told me I owned for so long. And I had lost it in front of my entire team.

We boys are taught real early that to be a boy means to take up space and to fight for space and to destroy whatever is in the way between us and our dreams. That day I lost mine. The way I saw it, DJ took it from me. A deep shame came over me—the kind you feel when you know you've failed and that you can't do anything about it. It was the shame of having to tell all the people back home, who always thought I was going to the NFL, why I wasn't playing at games, why my name wasn't being called. It was the shame of having no way to run and nowhere to hide from this failure.

Playing college sports, you learn how to see the person next to you as a friend but never too close. Each of your futures hang in the balance. It is a terrible way to live. It is a terrible way to grow up. It is a terrible way to learn how to love yourself. It is a terrible way to learn how to love others. But it is the way that I learned. You do what you have to do to prove that you belong where you do. To be Black and rural, and to find my body on a white campus with orange tiger paws, was to be forced to prove that my body mattered as much as the name on the back of my jersey.

I think for the first time that day I hated someone who was Black. I think for the first time I wanted to destroy someone who looked like me the same way I saw white people learning to destroy us. I think it was the first day that I finally wanted another Black person to fail in all the ways we read about. I wanted him to fail in all the ways our parents warned us not to. I wanted him to fail in all the ways that would harm his white protection and his white resources and his white celebration. I wanted him to fail in all the ways I knew I was failing and was afraid to admit.

This is how we learned to survive college: by distrusting one another. Distrust can be a powerful thing, especially when you learn to distrust those who look like you. You learn to view them with skepticism, as dangerous, always a threat of taking something from you. Was that the dynamic on the plantation? Black people who were trying to survive learned distrust. The white supremacist structure, both in the country and in the church, shaped the demand for it. It wasn't their fault. It was forced upon them. I learned that it is more than distrust; it is self-hatred.

Years later, I now realize that DJ and I were just alike. We both came from the bottom and were just trying to make good on the lessons that we'd learned early from our people. We were both trying to prove white people wrong about us. Every. Single. Day. We were trying to prove that we were the "good Black boys." So many friends and family back home would drop out of school. Some would get pushed out. Some would be ignored. Some would just leave. So we had to be good and much better than those "nig-gas" back home. We had so much to prove. That we could have perfect attendance. That we were studi-ous. That, in some sense, we were human. That's what it was: We were proving that our successful Black bodies were human Black bodies. We couldn't fail like the others, lest our parents be proven irre-sponsible. Other boys (that's who we are in college, really, children) stood as individuals and never as a reflection of their whole community. Us? No, we had to move differently. It's just horrible that our moves meant being more skeptical of ourselves than of the system that forces us against one another.

I really wish I would have learned to love DJ in-stead of distrusting him. I would have realized that our struggle was so much more than how well we could produce on the field, and that our struggle was not against each other, and that our struggle was to find ways to love and find ways to give up the lies we learned and find ways not to destroy ourselves and others in the process. I really wish I had learned that Black boys on white college campuses are not actu-ally adults but children in need of protection, in need of better lessons about being human, and being boys, and being vulnerable, and being willing to tell the truth about our pain, and being willing to stop hiding behind numbers, and finding pleasure together in simply just being, and winning, and losing, and learn-ing, and healing, and accepting ourselves, and finding beauty in ourselves, and worlds to be explored in our minds, and growing up without the fear of rejection, or prison, or punishment. I wanted us to give up the lies that good Black boys always make bad Black sentences.

But I learned that lesson too late.

Instead of seeking the truth, I kept running.

By that point, I'd become accustomed to hearing white praise from the white church I was attending. But now, desperate for affirmation and approval, desperate to prove my worth, I *ran* toward it. I thought I was just running toward good things, like community and church and God. But in reality I was sprinting far from my Black Pentecostal church, Black preaching, Black communities, where I'd have to face the truth of myself—and toward a very nice white Jesus.

The more I pursued white Jesus and his disciples, the more I learned about what felt like the "right" kind of Christianity. The more I learned how to get into arguments to pick apart someone else's experience. The more I learned to distrust others. Life, for me, was not about growing up and giving up lies and loving the person I saw in the mirror. It was about looking in the mirror, then walking away to be with people who invited me to live in proximity with them, yet never really seeking to know or truly love me. But I chased this community; it became the air I breathed. In honesty, it gave me a place where I really didn't have to face the shame of who I had become because it never called into question who I was becoming. It let me run from myself. It rewarded me for it.

It praised Black bodies singing white worship songs and tearing apart whatever Black people put out in the world. It was a place where I learned to be "Christian" and never to be Black. I began listening to sermons by John Piper, John MacArthur, and other big-name reformed pastors literally every single day. Listening to sermons became much easier than listening to myself.

Running became a way of escaping what I didn't want to face, what I didn't have words for, what I didn't realize was true of me. I embraced the teachings that told me to just lean and depend on Jesus and sing my heart happy and make good grades and learn white jokes and wear clean suits because that would make me matter.

AFTER I GRADUATED, JAS AND I GOT MARRIED AND moved to California, since she had entered the military and was stationed there. We both had to find home again.

For some reason, in so many conversations I'd have about Jesus, it never occurred to me that Jesus actually loved Black people, or that Black people actually knew Jesus, or that Black people got anything right about Christianity, for that matter. So when I moved out to California, I wasn't really looking for Black people or Black churches. I had learned that my real family and real community and the real Christianity came from the lips of those whose breath smelled like pour-overs and whose pants were ripped and who could quote old dead white guys better than they knew how to talk about Jesus. We realized there was a world much bigger than the rural country towns we grew up in. So when we moved out to California, we found ourselves a nice white mega-church where they served lattes and espresso.

A few weeks later, after having told myself that the way I was raised to practice my faith was wrong, I called my momma. She was so happy to hear about all the things I was experiencing under the blue California skies. I told her about all the black coffee I had been drinking. I told her about all the seasoned food from white folks I was eating. I told her about all the ways my legs hurt from running from my house to base and back again. I told her about all the ways I was happy about making it out and how the trees looked different and there was no white South Carolina dirt, and no whooping, and no long church services and no more midnight services to go to as the new year begin. I know she was hurt. I know she was hurt because I talked about all the good things I was experiencing with white people in the short time I'd been in California more than I talked about all the good things I had learned from Black people all my life.

"Hey, Ma," I said, "how you doing today?" She told me about everything she did that day as a nurse. She talked about all the kids she'd cared for. I told her about how I applied to a job and didn't get a call back. "It's going to be alright," she said, assuring me that maybe my name just got lost in the mix.

"Ma," I said.

"Yes," she responded.

I felt like a rock was in my throat. There was a long pause. "I think I want . . ." My mind went back to all the fiery sermons about not leaving the church and how I would go to hell if I did and how there's only one name under heaven by which we would be saved. "I think I want to get baptized again."

She paused.

I paused.

It was the type of pause that you take to gather yourself when you feel like a dagger has struck you.

"What do you need to get baptized for?" she asked. I could tell in her voice that she was getting aggravated.

"Ma, I just don't feel like I did it right as a kid," I said.

"What do you mean?" she said.

"Ma, that stuff y'all teach is all wrong," I said.

"All what is all wrong?" she asked, taken aback.

I begin to tell her all the ways the Black Pentecostals were wrong in all the ways that I had learned from white dudes with Bibles and microphones and podcasts. Eventually, I outright said to her: "I'm not Pentecostal anymore. I'm *reformed*."

Funny thing is neither of us really knew much about what that word meant. But in that conversation, I had cut deeper than I could ever imagine.

I was not just changing the way I talked, the way I dressed, the way I thought, the way I worshipped, the words I said. I was turning my back on her, and all the ways she loved us, and all the ways she tried to teach us not to fail, and all the ways she prayed and cried at night, and all the ways she endured arguments from white people about the ways mothers who look like her don't teach their kids how to be more moral, more excellent, and more silent.

I hung up the phone. She was hurt. She was angry. I didn't care. White people mattered more.

We didn't talk for a while.

WEEKS LATER, ON EASTER SUNDAY, THE LIGHTS WERE dim as the pastor walked around across the stage, back and forth, asking the congregation who wanted to be baptized. The smell of Febreze and coffee hung in the air—a completely different world from my childhood fellowship hall doused in the scent of perfumes and fried chicken. I raised my hand. I walked up to the stage to recommit my life to a new Jesus I hadn't known before.

They immersed my body in the water. When I came back up, I felt good. I was now clean. The people in the room started to clap their hands as the worship leader began to sing. My body was wet. I was hugged. I was cheered. I had become new. The old things had passed away.

This was perhaps the most emblematic moment of the way I learned to shut off parts of myself, lest I be that type of Black person. It was the lessons of survival that we learned. So much depended on our ability to, as the Bible says, die daily. It worked for me. Honestly, it granted me opportunities in places. I wasn't too much of a threat. I learned in these spaces that God was really only concerned about our souls and not really with the larger questions happening in society, at least not for us Black people. White people were granted that. White people were the *real* persecuted. They were the *real* people experiencing loss in this country. I believed the lies. The liberals were taking the country from them and we needed to do all that we could to save ourselves from them.

In my mind I was learning a lot of things. Since I was a kid I had always had a desire to learn, to know. So when I was handed a stack of books, written by mostly conservative white men, to me this was knowledge worth getting. I devoured the pages like cookies and cream ice cream on a hot summer day. I learned the language of whiteness, I learned what ministry looked like. I learned and I learned, and I didn't question it because what I was learning was giving me something in white spaces that has come by hard for Black folk: *access*. I never questioned it because as we all knew, white meant right, Black meant suspicion. White was just normal, Black meant danger. White was good and moral. But Black? Never good enough.

There was something about believing the myth of Black exceptionalism—that somehow I was different from *those* Black people—that I enjoyed so much. But it was dangerous. It was a weapon, used by me, used by other Black people, used by white people, always against Black people. Always.

The wages would come. But in the moment, all I could feel was the power.

THE BLACK SOCIOLOGIST W.E.B. DU BOIS SPEAKS OF the Veil of Color and double consciousness in his book *The Souls of Black Folk*. "One ever feels his twoness," he writes, "an American, a Negro; two souls, two thoughts, two unreconciled strivings; two warring ideals in one dark body." He spoke of our struggle in this country between being Black and seeing ourselves through the eyes of others. There is always this struggle: finding yourself in the world, always being seen, trying to see yourself. Some call us exceptional, speaking of how good it is for us to be around them, that somehow we passed through the veil that was torn when we gave up ourselves for them. Some others paternalize us. They believe themselves to be messiahs, saviors. Salvation means being disconnected from our people, from our community, and brought into the white family of God. "Between me and the other world," he writes, "there is an unasked question." It is unasked in all the assumptions, in all the blaming, and all the lies, and all the sentences that somehow make us believe Blackness should be demonized, and whiteness divinized. That question, Du Bois found out, was: How does it feel to be a problem?

That was the terrifying thing about what I had become. My body and my Blackness had become a problem, and I had let it. I had passed into the other world, the white world, and I had become free, and wet, and washed, and clean, and white as snow, and white as white folk desired me to become. Instead of seeing the "soul-beauty of a race which his larger audience despised," I saw the beauty of the opportunity of becoming the person that my larger audience had praised.

That day, when I went down dry and my body came back up wet, the waters bringing me into whiteness won. I came up new: I was not Black—I was Christian. At least that's what I was told: *My Christian identity was more important than my racial identity.* I just wish that was true when I walked out the church doors.

MIKE BROWN WAS MURDERED WHILE JAS AND I WERE in California. The Charleston shooting happened as well. I remember both. The cries that I heard from Black people as they tried to witness to the pain. The images that came across my screen, the faces of people who looked just like me, the faces of those who were murdered, the faces of those whose tears traveled across the country as they declared that Black Lives Matter. I remember it all. But I don't like what I remember about them.

I remember saying that Black people should not be protesting. I remember quoting white people's words over our dead Black bodies. I remember going to church and singing and never hearing the name Michael Brown. I remember riding in the car and telling my white friend that Black people are losing the gospel. I remember talking about all the ways I hated a Black man in the White House. I remember never saying rest in peace. I remember all of it. I remember not feeling a thing. I remember not feeling any pain. I remember not feeling any anger. I remember not feeling ashamed to harm myself, and harm my friends back home, and most of all harm my Black wife.

Jas was in tears when both murders happened. She was terrified. I was not. She was depressed. I was not. She was shook. I was not. She was confused by me. *How could her Black husband not feel anything? How could I see those precious faces and not feel a damn thing?* She'd cry to me, and I'd have nothing to say. And while she was crying in private, I was destroying Black people in public.

Though the events were months apart, they felt so, so close. Jas did not have time to recover. She was sad for months. She went to work sad. She came home sad. But I felt nothing. I didn't care. The gospel mattered more.

To many, Mike Brown was a criminal. To Jasmine, he was a prince, a friend, a child. When she cried all those tears, I had nothing. I had no consolation. I had no words. No hugs. I was cold. I had never seen her that sad, that moved. I had never seen her that angry. I had absolutely nothing.

I was too concerned about losing the position that I had in white churches. Too concerned about losing the praise that white people gave me. Too concerned about losing their love, and their hugs, and the chances to preach, and chances to lead, and chances to feel like I mattered. It was too much to give up. I was not willing to lose it. I was not willing to face all the ways I had learned to hate myself and hate my momma and hate Black boys in Florida and Ferguson, Missouri. I was not willing to face all the ways I had learned to fail, and to love white folk, and to distance myself from Black people, and to be cold, and to run, and to be ashamed, and to desire white praise. White people mattered more in that moment than my Black wife. White people mattered more in that moment than my Black momma. White people mattered more in that moment than Black pain. White people mattered more in that moment than Black life.

White supremacy was not just about terrible white American men in white hoods with white crosses. It was also about all the terrible ways I learned how to harm Black people and be terrible to Black people and not listen to Black people and not cry over Black people and not care about Black people and to do it all in the name of Jesus. I believed white people were the center of my world. I believed every other person's value was determined by them. I believed Black people must be the cause of our own pain, our death. I must make this confession: I was anti-Black. I found out that white people were not the only ones who could be cold and callous, complicit and complacent, in the project of white supremacy. A racist culture, as Ibram X. Kendi writes, had handed me the ammunition to shoot Black people, to shoot myself, and I took it and used it.

I don't tell this story to make myself feel better. It is hard as hell to write and to admit. I tell it because it is the truth. Truth is the beginning of liberation. It is the beginning of what we really want for ourselves as humans. It is what we are encouraged to be and become in our faith tradition. It is the beginning of life. Giving up our lies so that we can really love.

I learned how to lie.

I learned how to fail.

I learned how to hate.

I learned how to steal.

I learned how to harm.

And once I gave up the lies, about Black people, our place in this country, our bodies and our lives, white people and their power, America and what it does to us all—once I had the courage to face myself and others—then and only then, did I hear the words of Jesus when he says, "You will know the truth, and the truth will make you free."

I would have to learn not to harm.

I would have to learn not to steal.

I would have to learn not to hate.

I would have to learn not to fail.

I would have to learn not to lie.

TERROR.

They killed him. *They.* America. It. And whenever we forget and say the word *we*, it slices deep into our flesh. "Remember, nigger. Remember your place," is the national coda. I cried. You nestled in my arms. My poor child.

—IMANI PERRY

If you grew up in the Black Pentecostal church, there are certain things you never forget. The women in skirts to their ankles. Wednesday noonday prayer. The smell of fried chicken, green beans, and macaroni and cheese permeating the sanctuary. The praise breaks and testimonies, the stories of how we made it. The off-key singing and prayer lines and long sermons.

I'll never forget those midnight cries. During church conventions, we'd call them *locked in*. People who had been long gone—or, as the people said, *backslid*—came back to be covered again. It was not that they were lost; they were not. But it was that they had lost touch. Preachers preached. Dancers danced. We would shout all night. Bodies let loose all over those old green floors. Ecstatic speech took over tongues. We couldn't understand what they were saying, but we knew there was something. Though our native tongue found no entry, what took over them was the spirit of deliverance. Those bodies were free.

I remember when it happened to me, when I caught the Holy Ghost. Tears flowed down my face as I pressed, forced myself, into this speech. Later I'd learn that the technical term was *glossolalia*—the Divine reaches out, grabs hold of your body, and you become a witness. Your body becomes a witness.

"Son, you did it," the members of the church said as I danced across the church floors. "You spoke in other tongues." They brought me up front, off to the side of the offering table, in front of the steel podium, and handed me the old microphone, which I gripped, my hand sweaty and trembling. "What did the Lord do for you?" they asked.

I paused. I could feel the eyes on me. The room was hot. I was sweating. The microphone barely stayed in my hand from the sweat. The praise break music got quieter. I could see my momma covering her mouth like she was about to sneeze. She didn't sneeze. She was crying.

"He gave me the gift," I said. Before I could get out the rest, the church went up in roaring. The click track started again. The praise break started again. I took off, shouting again. My momma and auntie were shouting like I'd just scored a touchdown on Friday night. I had the gift. They rejoiced, all of 'em. I was *saved*.

After that, it was customary that one would be baptized, washed in the Blood. This was the first time I got baptized. I didn't learn too much about the doctrines or anything. I just knew that they told us that baptism changed us. Long before I had become a baptized disciple of whiteness, I had become a baptized baby of the Black church. When they led me to the cold water, I could feel my body shake. I was trembling but I was happy. I was saved. For them, when my body came back up wet, the white garments sticking to my body like swimming trunks, this meant I was *really* saved. I could sing in the choir. I could wear those white gloves as I led people to their seat. I could play the drums. I could preach my sermon. I could be free. I could be free the way that I saw Black folk in all the documentaries my momma made us watch. I could be free without thinking about all the documentaries my momma made us watch. I could be human and free and normal. Or so I thought.

My siblings, Depaul, Dion, and Dominique, and I would always ride together wherever we went. Depaul was the oldest, muscular, his hair naturally wavy. Dion was next, skinny, fit, his hands fat like my daddy's. Dominique was next, short, athletic, a gap in her teeth, caramel brown skin. Then it was me. Depaul always had to make sure we made it wherever we were going. He was, whether by choice or by love, responsible for making sure we learned how to act straight, think straight, sit straight. He was to learn responsibility. We were to learn obedience. All of us were meant to make it. All of us were meant to survive the journey.

I always loved it when he drove. That meant I could listen to what my parents called the *bad* music. The church I grew up in made sure we weren't stained by the world, and by bad music, and by bad Black boys with their saggy pants and loud music, and bad Black girls and too much of their skin showing. He played Tupac and Bone Thugs-N-Harmony and Mark Morrison and Outkast and Trina and Missy Elliot. As the songs would skip, he would tell Dion to take the CD out and wipe it off with his spit-moist shirt. He'd put it back in the system of our silver eighties Oldsmobile Cutlass. I can still smell the old leather seats. I can still look up and see the upholstery of the ceiling coming loose. Depaul drove like it was his. Nothing made us happier than being in a car, together, listening to bad music, missing cracks in country back roads, bobbing our heads as our eyes saw fields, and then old trailers, and then an old church, and then more fields, and more old trailers, and more old churches.

Weeks later, after I had officially been saved, my siblings and I, as well as my cousin Josh, were on our way to my aunt's house to celebrate the graduation of one of our cousins. We always took the back way. We had traveled this road many times. Red dirt from the roads would cover the bottom of the old silver Cutlass. My momma fussed at us, really Depaul, but really us, too, all the time about driving that way. Depaul never really cared because that was the quickest way to get from our house to my grandmother's. As Depaul drove, he decided to stop on the shoulder of the road, which was barely the shoulder of the road because we were in rural South Carolina. He got out of the car to fix something. To our right was an old trailer home. A garden was to the right of the house. The porch had been added, run-down, brick with old broken white buckets on it. In front of us was woods and road. Behind us, more woods and more road.

An old white man came out of the house and stood on the porch, about thirty feet away. He started yelling something at my brother and us. Apparently he thought we'd thrown some trash in his yard. These yells were not just the yells of someone who was bothered by something. These yells were chilling.

They were the yells of someone who hated. They were the yells that we'd been warned to get as far away from as we could if we heard it. They were the yells of someone who wanted to ruin us.

My cousin Josh yelled to my brother Dion, "Put the window down, put the window . . ." My brother rushed to try and turn the knob. I heard no sounds.

I could tell something was going on that was not right. My body got cold. My heart started to race. I could feel my palms getting wet. I was afraid. "You be here when I get back!" the old man yelled, and he rushed into his house. Depaul returned some words to him and ran back to the car, jumped in, and started to speed off. The anxiety—nah, more than that: the *terror* took over my body when suddenly—

Bang.

Bang.

Bang.

He shot at us. My brother. My sister. My cousin. Children.

I could barely catch my breath. The first thing I knew to do was to run down my body to make sure I wasn't hit. My hands trembled as I patted my body. My sister was crying. Depaul was cursing. We were all afraid. I was confused. Why did he shoot at us? Why did he want to kill us? Why am I so afraid? Why can't I stop shaking? I cannot remember what happened next. It was all a blur. I was too terrified. My hands wouldn't stop trembling. I think I screamed. I think we all screamed. I know what we all felt: terror. Why did he want to ruin us?

We made it home that day. But my hands wouldn't stop trembling. My body wouldn't stop shaking. My palms were still wet.

Weeks later, we pressed charges. My momma and my daddy told the police how terrified they were, and how terrified we had been. How they could have lost their children, and how hatred was still alive, and how sad they were for this town, and how sad they were that this moment would burn in our eyes and in our hearts and in our bodies. When my momma walked into our small-town courthouse, she could overhear the cop talking with the assailant through the paper-thin walls. She heard the cop say to him, "This what happens when they don't keep they children in they place."

They. That's how both Black folk and white folk in South Carolina say "their." But *their* they and *our* they meant two entirely different things. I could feel the force of that word when she said that. *They* had power to rewrite reality. *They* justified all the myriad of ways both white men and white cops harmed us. *They* justified calling Black parents niggers in the most sophisticated ways possible. *They* thought they knew us, but they didn't know us at all.

And for our purposes in that courthouse on that

day, *they* carried the full force of white lies and white innocence and white terror against rural Black families in rural Black towns.

The judge didn't believe us. The judge did not believe us at all. Any of us. *They.*

Our testimony meant nothing to him. They heard our stories, even found the man's guns. But it was not enough.

My soul was saved, but not my body.

No amount of prayers could save it. No amount of Sunday school lessons, math problems, orange jerseys, and letters behind my name could save it from American terror. This lesson haunted me from the day I heard the shots ring out from the gun of a white man who wanted to ruin us. My body was not saved.

NEITHER WAS IT SAVED WHEN, IN 2012, I FOUND MY-self lost in Greenville one night, after I had gone to see one of my friends play a gig at a bar. It was a good night. Cold, chilly. As I walked out of the bar, I could feel the southern chill touch me, penetrating the cover of my Clemson hoodie. I was headed back to Clemson in my black '95 Honda Accord with tinted windows, trying to find my way to U.S. Route 123 to get home, when I noticed a police car following me. I had passed the cop car just a few minutes before. I tried to do everything I could to appear normal, like I belonged where I was driving. I approached a cul-de-sac, came to a stop, put my car in reverse, and backed out to go the way I came. The cop followed me through the neighborhood. Then it happened. The blue lights came on. A part of me thought the cop had gotten a call and was about to speed by me. The cop did not. The cop was stopping me.

My hands started to tremble. I looked to the left. I looked out of my rearview mirror. *Do I got anything in the car?* I asked myself. I knew I didn't but the thought of it being so late and me being so alone and the blue lights catching the glare in my mirrors had me stressed. I could feel my palms get sweaty the same way my palms got sweaty when the man shot at us. My mind went away from the inside of my Honda that smelled like wet and stank cleats and french fries I just got from the bar. Some streetlights were out. Some were on. I didn't know none of the house numbers I saw. I didn't know any of the names of the streets I drove by. I slowed my car down.

I put the car in park. *My seat belt's on,* I said to myself. *Got my wallet. Registration. Aite.* I turned every light on in my car that I could. I put my hands on the steering wheel. I made sure I was still. I glanced over at the passenger seat to make sure the tiger paw on my jacket was visible, and made sure the tiger paw on my student card would be one of the first things the cop would see.

My heart began to race. It was late, around ten-thirty P.M. I was alone. I was terrified.

"Can I have your driver's license and registration?" the cop said, as he shined his flashlight in my car, finally approaching my black Honda.

"Yessir," I responded. My hands were shaking. I could barely take it out. I handed him my license and my registration, along with my student ID, so that he would know that I didn't mean any trouble. My momma always told us that if we were stopped by the cops, we had to do everything that we could to make it home. "Just make it home," she would say. "Just make it home."

The officer took a look at my ID cards.

"What are you doing here?" he asked. "Do you know where you are? Do you know why I stopped you?" he asked.

"No, sir," I responded. "I'm just trying to get home."

"You were driving suspicious," he said.

I don't know what it meant to be driving suspiciously when you are lost. I was just trying to make it home. I was trying not to make any wrong turns. I was making sure that my name didn't end up in bad sentences. So, I drove slowly. I made frequent stops.

When he was asking me questions, he kept alluding to the area we were both in as one of high crime and drugs. He told me that cars like mine were suspicious in the area. He told me that I shouldn't be there.

"Wait in the car," he said, saying that he would be back. "Stay still."

I wondered if he'd caught a glimpse of my Clemson ID. I wondered if he could see the fear in my face, in my hands as they held on to the wheel. I wondered if he heard the cracks in my voice as I told him that I was just trying to get home.

I wanted him to see my name on my jersey. I wanted to tell him I was having some good spring ball sessions. I wanted to do anything I could to make this a quick and easy stop.

But another cop pulled up. Then another. Then another. His blue lights were still shining and illuminating the back of my black Honda. They kept me there for what seemed like hours. Looking all in my black Honda and all over my Black body.

As I waited in the car, I called my mom. "Ma," I told her, "a cop pulled me over." She asked me what for. All the other times that I got pulled over—and I would call her like she told me to do every time I got pulled over—I would tell her the reason. I'd rolled through a stop sign; I'd been over the speeding limit. But this time I had none.

"He said that I was looking suspicious and that I shouldn't be in this area." I put my mother on speakerphone. "Ma," I told her, "I'm scared."

She immediately began instructing me on how to maneuver my body.

"Keep your hands where they can see them," she said, distress in her voice.

"I am."

"Don't look any other way, keep your hands on the wheel," she said.

"I am," I said.

My hands were sweaty. One of the cops came to the right side of my vehicle and shined his light in my car. "Ma," I said in a soft voice, "he's shining his flashlight in my car." She told me to stay still and don't say nothing. I could hear her start to pray. It was like a mumble. She started to call on the name of Jesus and prayed that God was true to the word and that the hedge of protection was around me.

After half an hour, the officer returned to my vehicle. I wondered what took him so long. And why this other cop was looking in my car. Most of all, I wondered how I would get home. I was hoping that none of them would ask me to exit my car. I was hoping that my momma would stop praying, and that my heart would stop racing, and my bladder would not feel like it was full of Gatorade and butterflies. I knew they were not just armed with bullets. They were armed with a fear that called into question my ability to get lost and to find my way and just make it home. They were armed with much more than authority. They were armed with an ability to stop my car and stop my future. So I was afraid. I was terrified. My palms couldn't stop sweating. My stomach couldn't stop churning.

"Mr. Stewart," he said. "With a vehicle like yours, you don't want to be driving out here this late. Your car looked suspicious. Your car is the type of car that drug dealers drive. I had to make sure you wasn't a drug dealer," he explained. "You're free to go." He handed me back my information, and the other officer returned to his vehicle.

None of it made sense.

I didn't understand it then, but now I know that my life was caught between my mother's prayers and their suspicion. The moment became a testimony for my momma because her child lived—and for those officers, this was just another day trying to stop black cars that look suspicious. For me, this moment was not just another day. It meant to be Black in the presence of white people who thought I was suspicious and could think that way for no other reason than their belief in their right to police what they didn't believe was normal.

My momma and my dad would always tell us about all the ways they used to be terrified. For them—one a baby of the fifties and the other a baby of the sixties—it meant trying to forget how terrible white people could be, how terrible the country would let them be, and how terrifying it was for them as children to hear over the radio waves, "Martin is dead." They remembered Medgar being murdered, his wife and children seeing his Black body in the driveway and his dead Black body in the hospital. They remember Malcolm, and all the ways that he told them that they were Black and somebody, and

the terrible experience of learning that his voice had
been silenced as the hot lead entered his flesh. They
remember Fred, and his fist in the air, and his small
afro, and his audacious sermons, and his young life
vanishing before their very eyes. They remember the
cruelty. They remember that Black people's calls for
justice were not met with open arms, circles of
prayers, and worship songs to Jesus. It was met by
more brutality, beating what little love was left in us.

Sometimes I try to talk to my dad about back
then. Every time I do, I can see his mood change; his
whole body seems to be shook at the possibility of
revisiting such horror stories. I had breakfast with
him one morning. I knew that I wanted to talk about
what it meant for him to grow up in rural South
Carolina. We would talk about football and comput-
ers and Bruce Lee movies. We could talk until our
food got cold. But when I wanted to talk about Dil-
lon, South Carolina, he never wanted to say much
about it. The only thing I've really been able to get
out of him is "My dad was preaching during civil
rights," and "It takes everything not to hate white
people." I felt that when he said it. Maybe their forgetting is trying to protect themselves. To remember
the worst that happened to them was a terrible experience. So just like me, they got real good at lying
about how they were past all the terrible things white
people had done. They got real good at lying and not
telling us the truth about those white people still

being around and still terrorizing and how we would not be saved by running fast, and jumping high, and going to church, and keeping our hands on the steering wheel, and showing how deserving of life we were. I couldn't blame them. Lying is not always bad, especially when lying protects what little peace you have in the face of terror. But then maybe their forgetting was protecting me, saving me and white people from the rage that they know is possible. Being both Black and American, you get used to that. Maybe they were trying to get me to realize that only white bodies are allowed to be angry in this country, even violent, and still live to tell the story.

Me, nah. I had to be *careful,* lest I give off the wrong vibe, the wrong movement, the wrong look, the wrong car, the wrong body. Lest they have to attend a funeral instead of a graduation. Lest someone call my athletic frame suspicious. Lest someone shoot at me again and not miss. Lest their prayers go unanswered. Lest their lessons fall on deaf ears. Lest I never make it home. They always did that. They taught me: *This country, our country, judges us differently. My body was* judged *differently.* I was Black trying to prove that I am American.

I REMEMBER THE FIRST TIME I SAW A DEAD BLACK BODY: Friday, July 9, 2010. Swansea, South Carolina.

My uncle, the affectionate Ulysses Lykes, Sr., as

he would call himself, was the type of uncle that you bragged about to other people when they talked about their uncles. He would always show up to our house or my uncle's house next door; sometimes he had a drink in his hand, sometimes he didn't. Always joking and laughing, making fun of himself and others. His missing teeth would show as he cracked a smile, the smell of liquor on his breath, a terrible but familiar smell. His jawbones were strong, the white beard wrapped around his rough, dark chin. In his eyes were the colors red, off-white, and a deep brown as dark as his skin. I used to sing in church and he would always be talking about how well I sang, the ways I threw my hands on my hip, and threw my head back. He called it magic. He called it the real thing. He said I really had the anointing. He would pop in and out of church. When he did show up, I could tell he was honest about his faith. He would sing along with everyone, his breath still smelling like off-brand beer and mouthwash. Sometimes he would show up in colorful suits. Sometimes he would show up with a polo, black jeans, his hands polka-dotted from the painting he did that day. He was trying to walk, trying to battle the parts of himself that he had gotten used to covering just like the paint covered his hands. Like the paint on his hands, he never could quite cover enough to keep his rough skin, his deep scars, from showing.

He got real good at lying like I got real good at

lying. Sometimes his lies made him come to the altar, his shirt pressed to his back, the imprint of sweat looking like abstract art. Sometimes his lies made him sit alone, his liquor in one hand, his depression in the other, his heart shattered, his body bent. I could see him now, moving his body, throwing his hands around like he was conducting a choir. Unc and I would joke as well about how funny we thought it was that he could run so much in life but look like he had it all together. He had been broken in this country. He, like me, had grown up in the American South, the Black rural South. But his American South was able to do things to him that my American South only dreamed of. His American South was able to bend and break him in ways that it would be bent and broke if it dared do that to me. So, we laughed. About singing. About wounds. About football. About nothing. About us. About life. Before he would leave, he would always tell me something serious, some type of lesson a sage would leave the young student that would keep them living. He was so proud that I was at Clemson playing football.

"Boyyyyyyyyyy, you gonna be playing this year?" I ain't really want to answer that 'cause I wasn't playing too well. I didn't want to tell him about the ways I had learned to run on the field and run away from myself. I didn't want to tell him about how I felt my name was making bad sentences. I didn't want to tell him that I was about to lose my spot to DJ. I didn't want to tell him that I was afraid. I didn't want to tell him I wanted to destroy DJ the same way my uncle talked about white people destroying so many Black people in American schools and American businesses, on American fields, in American courtrooms, on American dirt roads, and on American streets.

"Yeah, Unc. I might." He didn't know nor did he care to know whether I was lying or not. He was just proud that somebody had finally "made it out." He was proud that in between cold drinks and warm mouthwash, he could tell somebody about the way his nephew made good on the lesson.

One morning, I was at church with my cousins practicing for Sunday worship. Unc was there—I remember the smile he gave me from a distance. Way off in the distance. His missing teeth, not saying a word, smiling.

Hours later, we received the call. Unc had gotten in a wreck just around the corner from the house. My body felt sick. I don't think I truly remember the sadness I felt deep in my bones that day, the grief that I felt travel from my head to the earth my feet were standing on. Our family rushed to the scene. My cousin Olivia, talking through tears, told me that she would pick me up and take me there. I don't think I was ready. I was terrified. Minutes later her red Honda pulled into my driveway. I got in. We sped down the road. We passed my great-grandmother's house; the open fields with old cars and old sheds

were still. The air felt like suffocation as the South
Carolina heat beat against the cracked roads. The
closer we got, the more cars lined the road. I could
tell it was not good. My aunts were holding their
children, shielding their eyes from what they saw. My
uncles were holding their mother, as she wept harder
and deeper than anything I had seen in my life. I ex-
ited the car. There he lay: *lifeless.*

We got to the scene before the medics and coro-
ner arrived. I couldn't believe what I was seeing. I
couldn't believe that his red Ford Explorer now
looked like a child's toy, crushed, pieces missing. Parts
of the car lay scattered in the road, parts of it were on
the shoulder of the road, parts of it were still pieced
together. His body, the body that had been bent and
broken in life, lay before all of our eyes bent and broken in death. It felt surreal but I couldn't help but
look. I couldn't help but try to hold on to what pieces
of his life still remained. As I stared at him, my mind
immediately went back to all the memories that we
shared. I couldn't have those anymore. He was gone.
No more laughing. No more missing teeth. No more
dancing. No more liquor-smelling breath. No more
lessons. No more running. No more nothing. He
was gone. I don't know when I became conscious of
my fear of death. I knew death is the journey we
must all take. But in that moment, there was something particularly terrorizing: the loneliness. He died
alone. Only to have others gather to see his mangled

flesh. And to try to hold on to what pieces of him we had in our hearts. Even writing about this makes me sad, because I can feel those feelings of loss that I felt that day. That was one of the first times I realized that one day that would be my body. I, too, would be a dead Black body.

I REMEMBER THE SECOND TIME I SAW A DEAD BLACK body. Tuesday, July 5, 2016. It was night.

I was leaving work at Enterprise Rent-A-Car that day. By this time, my wife and I had gotten stationed in Augusta, Georgia. We were back in the South. I always called my wife on the way home.

After we spoke, I made my way to church for midweek Bible study. The members of the church didn't call it *midweek Bible study,* but I did since that's what we called it in my Pentecostal church every time we came to the building and the day wasn't Sunday.

I checked my phone while I was waiting at the stoplight. My social media feeds were flooded with a video of a man in a red polo, with a wrinkled white T-shirt underneath. His haircut reminded me of the cuts that my brother would give all my cousins when he became the hood barber. His cheeks were pronounced, his teeth gold and his gap as wide as his lips when he smiled. This man's shirt was oversized, the same way we used to wear oversized white shirts with denim Girbauds, trying to see whose color-coded straps matched, like we were our own fashion show. Khaki shorts, probably to hold his wallet, some extra candy, and cash from selling bootleg CDs and DVDs that day—he'd done that all the time for the past two years.

As Alton Sterling was packing up for the day in front of the Triple S Food Mart, Baton Rouge police officer Howie Lake arrived on the scene. He confronted Alton for doing what he and so many others have been trying to do for a long time: trying to get it how you live, trying to make something of what little you had. Officer Blane Salamoni arrived to help Lake. They didn't lean on their training of de-escalation; they were trained to see big Black bodies as dangerous Black bodies. They carried in them the story that the country carried in it. They carried in them the story of hatred, rage, terror, and suffocation. They carried in them the same commitment to ruin. Seconds later, guns were drawn.

"Don't fucking move or I'll shoot your fucking ass, bitch. Put your fucking hands on the car," Salamoni shouts, never really interested in learning the name of this big Black body. "I'll shoot you in your fucking head. Don't you move. Put your hands on the fucking car," as he points the barrel of his black gun in the temple of Alton's Black head.

As I watch this, my body gets hot. Deep in my insides is a void. It is a darkness. I am more than sad.

I am more than terrified. I am more than in pain. I am engulfed with a burning as hot as that summer day when my uncle died.

"Alright man, you're hurting my arm," Alton responded, clearly distressed. My hand trembles. You could hear the tears welling up from him. I could feel the tears welling up in myself as I knew how this story would end, and I knew I couldn't do anything to stop it or save him or set him free. We are taught not to get on the cops' bad side because on their bad side means that our families would have to hold us in their memories and not in their arms.

They tase him. One officer tackles him into the front bumper of the silver Toyota. I remember hits like that. It was a defenseless hit. He wasn't prepared for it. He didn't even curl his body like we would on the field. He was blindsided.

I hear his breath. He's breathing hard, as the body camera goes around and around.

Seconds later: *Bang. Bang. Bang. Bang. Bang.*

Alton's big Black body gasps for the last breaths before his parting journey. Instead of the customary *ashes to ashes, dust to dust,* Officer Salamoni's eulogy to Alton? "Stupid motherfucker."

Even in Alton's last moments, as he bled out alone, his red shirt showing dark bloodstains, this white boy with a badge believed the lie: Alton's death was Alton's fault. To Blane Salamoni, this dead Black body was a stupid Black body.

. . .

I SAT STUNNED. I HATED EVERY BIT OF THE VIDEO. I still remember until this day the sight of his lifeless, dead body, filled with bullets. I can see him now, his body unmoving. My body? I could feel the cold, empty void in my insides. The taste in my mouth was raw.

For the longest time I had learned to shut off parts of myself, to stay composed in the white evangelical church. I didn't want to become the trope of the *angry Black dude*. From my beginnings of being with white Christians at Clemson to now being in my church in Augusta, I had learned how to laugh at jokes that I didn't get, talk about movies that I didn't know, imitate preachers that I didn't really understand. All through our lives we heard lectures about anger, how it made you selfish, a distraction, how it was unprofessional, even un-Christian. So we learned real good how to either cover our ignorance, our pain, and our shame, or simply just escape.

That night, though, that night when Alton's Black body entered the space where I sat, a weight within me sank deep. I couldn't run. I couldn't escape the weight, the overcoming sadness that I felt deep in my stomach as it churned and churned at the thought of a body like mine lifeless all over social media. I didn't know what to do with it. A part of me was hungry, but most of all I was numb. It was a deep, abiding numbness that feels but doesn't feel, that thinks but doesn't think. The type of numb that makes your mouth dry, each swallow seemingly never making it to your chest and then to your stomach. I was both terrified and sick.

Inside my truck, now in the church parking lot, I began to yell. I couldn't escape the fear, the anger, the sadness. So I tried to compose myself. Tried not to show how sad I was.

I walked into church. I told one of the members what happened, what I was feeling. I was given the nod like they heard me but really didn't.

"It's good to see you, Stew," someone else said.

"Yeah," I said, "good to see you, too."

"How's your day?" he said.

It took me a moment to respond. "I'm aite," I said.

My face wasn't showing the smile it usually had. My body wasn't bouncy. I felt dull, and I knew I looked it, too. I was numb.

Yet I was there. I still showed up because this was my church, this was my family, this was my home.

We gathered into our seats as the worship service began. "In Christ Alone . . ." the congregation started to sing, in their normal southern bluegrass. As I looked around me, I felt a sort of coldness and loneliness that I hadn't felt before. I looked, panning the space; I was surrounded by a sea of white faces. I was always aware of it, but something felt different. Like I had a reason to notice what this might have meant. As I looked around the church, it wasn't just that I didn't see people who looked like me. It was that I didn't see the sadness, the anger, the rage that was crying out in my body.

I didn't see us, I didn't feel us, I didn't hear us.

We were invisible.

LATER THAT WEEK, THE WEEK THAT ALTON WAS MURdered, I said some words about how I was feeling on Facebook. Social media for me became a way to write about what I was feeling. I didn't feel like I could talk. I didn't feel like I could say what I wanted to say in public. But I knew I could write. I resolved to express a small part of the deep sadness I felt— while staying safe and committed to white Christians. "I'm very confident," I wrote, "that God will lead the hearts of our congregation."

The responses immediately rolled in.

"Jesus doesn't see color," one member of my church replied.

"Jesus sees us all the same," said another.

Funny thing is, not too long ago, I believed that. I believed that Jesus didn't see color and I believed that Christians shouldn't see color, either. So when the members wrote that on my post, I didn't know how to respond. I had no idea how to make them feel what I felt inside of me.

I didn't want to cause any drama, so I acquiesced and went with it. "I agree," I said. "Jesus doesn't see color. . . . The gospel unites us and makes us one."

We had been members of the church a few months by then. I had gotten used to hearing bluegrass worship songs, talking sports with men in khaki shorts and polos, talking about the latest book by reformed pastors that I had read. The sermons were short. Every Sunday was filled with pastors dropping quotes from old dead white guys, and living white guys in white churches, talking about white schools, and writing white books.

The week after Alton was murdered, our sermon series began to explore marriage. Week after week, we heard about what God wanted us to do in our singleness, and what God wanted us to reflect in our marriages, and the grace of God for our sins, and the forgiveness of God for our failures.

Not once during any of those Sundays—or any Sundays thereafter—was there any mention of Alton's name. Never did the sins named include a country that did not know God but did know violence. None of it mentioned what we were going through. We were being taught, week in and week out, how to be Christian. But we were not being taught how to live in America.

. . .

"DO YOU WANT TO PREACH IN THE UPCOMING WEEKS?" the pastor asked me. It was two months after Alton was murdered. It was two months after many of the white members had responded to Alton's death like it was a passing day. I was an intern, and he said he wanted to give me and others opportunities to preach. Of course I accepted. I was happy to have the opportunity to do what I used to do in my home church. I was happy—really happy—that the gift I knew was inside of me would once again be able to come out.

I went out and bought a suit for the occasion. It was special. Jas told me how good the blue suit, white shirt, and skinny black tie that I purchased from H&M looked. I told my momma all about my excitement. I told my friends. "I'm ready," I told myself as I nervously pored over my notes of the sermon, my breath smelling like the black coffee and fried eggs that I had earlier that morning. I was going to preach on unity. John 17. I had written an essay earlier that month as I tried to deal with what I was feeling. I had really believed that coming together would solve all of our problems. I believed that America was far worse than I had ever known it to be—but I also believed that a message on unity was what we needed to help me feel human, white people less racist, the church more equal, and the country more loving.

I took the stage. I fumbled to open up my Bible with my notes that had scribbled writing on them about how terrified I had been. I looked down at my Bible. I looked up at the crowd. I looked around the church. I prayed my prayer, taking a glance at the crowd, seeing those who just earlier that week talked all over my social media about how race is not a problem, and how the church is the answer, and how America is the greatest country on earth, and how unity is what we needed. I preached, for I knew it would make me feel good, make the white members feel better, make the few Black members feel seen, and make all of us feel special, as if we weren't touched by death all around us. But for the first time, I realized: *This is not home.*

Within this particular church life, a sort of constant triumphal story would hang in the air, in the books we read, in meetings around the dinner tables, and in talk among small groups. We breathed in the story that the images of the dead we were seeing were somehow isolated incidents, that somehow it was just individual people with individual problems that didn't reflect the rest of the country. We exhaled, from our lips, a gasp of safety, like running in a horror story, finally having the assurance that we were safe. I believed them. At least I wanted to believe them enough not to lose what little I had there. It wasn't so much that *we* were safe around them, but that I had become safe *for* them. Safe because I didn't really make too much noise about the larger things that were going on in society.

They had gotten used to my safety during the two years that Jas and I were members there. I did, too. I had spent years in white churches showing that I was the nice Black dude.

The silhouette of a successful Black body was no longer just a shadow of a figure; I had become that person. I had become a *symbol of racial progress*. Graduated college, married, working, ascending the heights of whiteness, critical of people who looked like me, and never, ever saying those godforsaken words *white supremacy*. I had once again passed through the veil that my childhood church, First Baptist, created. I had once again become one of those types of Black people—who, ironically, are mostly Black men, who learn the language of theology, high concepts, going on shooting dates, being a "man's man," drinking black coffee, polos and denim jeans, books, stacks of books, performing our Blackness through charismatic gesturing, part whooping, part theorizing, and topped with the subtle but not so subtle anti-Blackness, the subtle but not so subtle misogyny, the subtle but not so subtle arrogance.

That's the danger of erasure: I never quite asked myself what I was losing in the process, and what and who was getting hurt. I didn't even realize it. It wasn't my fault, because both my parents and this country told me that proximity to whiteness would save me, our parents, and our country. I never questioned any of it because I learned that talking about race, or better yet, talking about being Black in this country, is not helpful and good, but only a distraction from the real task at hand: getting a degree, getting a job, getting a family, and not causing too much trouble— trouble with white people, that is.

But once the country witnessed Alton's murder, the scales began to fall from my eyes. Soon, whether I was preaching on Sundays or leading groups during weekdays, I was reminded of that lonely, empty void I felt the night I saw that Alton was murdered. That empty void stayed in my body.

Jasamine and I spent the next few weeks processing and finding ways to name all that felt near impossible to name. The weeks stretched into a long summer, which grew into a year that felt as endless as it was jarring. We had believed, like so many Americans believed, that things were getting better, that there was the hope of a new America, that the election of President Barack Obama marked the turning of a page, that the country was learning to grow up, that the church was the place of hope, and that all the terrible things that were happening around us were a part of God's cosmic plan for better. There were hopes held out; that was the language that so many people used: *hope.*

And then, we woke up. Some had been awake for decades; I joined far too late. Black Lives Matter woke many of us up to see the reality that the Black freedom struggle had never ended. To see the truth that white supremacy had never died; it just evolved and became deeper and harder to destroy because so much of our country depended on it staying alive.

For too long, I'd see Black faces in white pulpits; Black coaches at white universities, Black artists and celebrities all over white networks, Black millionaires and Black billionaires. I thought the message was clear: Race was behind us. But the reality for me set in with the cruelest force: Black people were still being murdered at alarming rates, Black people were still left behind economically, our children's schools were still disregarded, our lives were still in danger. Black people were still in a country and in churches that neither knew how to reform themselves, nor how to give up the lies they so tightly held on to, and actually love us and themselves enough to care for our suffering. The message became clearer: White supremacy was still our greatest sin and our deepest delusion.

I COULDN'T RUN ANYMORE. I DID NOT WANT TO DEAL with what it would mean for Alton's body to become a mirror to see both myself in him and what the country thought and had done to both of us. He had become a mirror for me to see how tired I was of lying—of how profound my delusion was, and how little it protected me. He became a mirror for me to see how tired I was of performing, and preaching,

and singing, and doing whatever would keep me secure around white Christians. I didn't want to admit
that being around white Christians became a way to
hide and to run from all the lessons my parents taught
me. I didn't want to be honest about how terrified I
was. And yet I was. And when my eyes beheld Alton,
I could not run.

I often wonder what the trauma of being forced to
endure such cruelty does to us. We have normalized
images and videos of dead Black children, women, and
men taking flight across social media. It has become
quite routine. It is a story as old as America. A national
story. It is a story that we have been forced to deal with.
Enslaved Black bodies became dead Black bodies. Hy-
persexualized Black bodies became dead Black bodies. Dangerous Black bodies became dead Black bodies.
Segregated Black bodies became dead Black bodies. Ed-
ucated Black bodies became dead Black bodies. In-
carcerated Black bodies became dead Black bodies.
Playful and prayerful Black bodies became dead Black
bodies. Black bodies marching in the street, preaching the good news of Jesus, fighting for the right to
vote, making lyrics and love songs: America made
sure that they became dead, never to sing, never to
love, never to dance, and never to rise again.

Terror.

You know neither the day nor the hour—as the
old Pentecostal leaders would tell us—when one can
be met by violence. And the fact that we are still here

is no testament to the goodness of the country. We are not here because our country, and the people of this country, have been exceptional at becoming more loving, and more honest, and less violent. No, we are here because we refused to believe their lie that our lives don't matter, and that we should accept our suffering, and the best parts of ourselves are what can survive whiteness and terror.

Still, the white country, as James Baldwin called it, doesn't know what to do with its *niggers*. For it invented the nigger, by making itself white and infusing the stigma of color into its schools, its county lines, its ballot boxes, its precincts, its churches, its community, and even in the ironically named White House. It snatched sons from their mothers, daughters from their fathers, and believed it was God's precious gift to do so without consequences. Now it must rid itself of the nigger, lest the nigger actually tell the truth of this country: that this country, and its white countrymen, are violent. White bodies with badges, white bodies with gavels, white bodies with Bibles, white bodies with bullets, must rid themselves of Black bodies because they believed the lie that the source of their problems was Black bodies being free bodies.

There is a part of the story of our country that rewards dead Black bodies.

Slave catchers would receive rewards for catching Black bodies on the loose, trying to find a place to be free. Ordinary white people forcefully got the country they desired, one in which signs not only gave them rights over other people, but one in which they believed that the place of the Black body was either dead, beneath, or caged. Even today, white bodies with badges get paid administrative leave while Black bodies receive the reward of burned metal and hot lead, babies in the spotlight, sharing all the wonderful memories, mothers and fathers having to live the grief and relive the trauma when the next dead Black body replaces your baby's dead Black body in the news cycle. The next child, the next woman, the next man who become hashtags were never meant to hold out hopes, nor were they ever meant to be in prayers, nor were they ever meant to be in history books; they were never meant to be mirrors—a chance for this country to look at itself and the way that it treats its Black citizens. They were more than that. They were meant to be the beautiful humans they were. They were meant to live in a place where we could see the best of ourselves and the worst of ourselves. They were meant to be loved. They were meant to be held. They were meant to just simply be. That is what we were to see.

What would the country see? What would the church see as the people who claimed to love Jesus's body were the same people claiming that Black bodies deserved to be cruci-fied bodies? Both would see what Salamoni and Lake saw, and what those other police officers that night saw, and the white man who shot at us saw: Black people not deserving to be free and be loved and be human.

When I think about Alton right now, and when I remember the white officer's ode to his Black body, I see now it was more than sadness that I felt—it was terror. It was terror because his beautiful Black body was not saved. He was so worthy of love, of being able to grow up, of being able to find delight in selling the latest Drake or J. Cole track, of selling films of poor quality with people walking across the screens, of making mistakes, of being seen, of being protected, of having a future.

The terror remains.

I PASSED A BROTHER THAT LOOKED LIKE ME, A BLACK body like mine, in a heated interaction with the cops this morning. It was tense. There were four cops around him. I stopped. Others stopped. We all put our hazard lights on. Some of us started recording, lest this Black brother have no one fighting for him. Every last one of us who stopped were Black. We know what Black boy bodies and white boy bodies with badges and bullets could mean for any of us. We knew, one by one, that we couldn't keep driving. I will not forget the terror I saw over one mother's face, when I looked in her eyes as she fumbled to grab something from the middle console. I will not forget the anger I saw in the brother's eyes as he was questioned by multiple cops, arguing his case. I saw it. I felt it. He made it out alive. I'm so glad he made it out alive. But I know he's wounded. I know his wings were clipped. I know his feet were tied. But he made it.

After I left the scene, I couldn't help but think of my son, my beautiful baby boy. I could not help but think of the deep fear—as deep as the memories that I lock in the crevice of my mind—that has taken over me since he was born. It is abiding. From time to time I hold him, I hold his flesh tightly, and write poems and Psalms to him, trying to let my heart become a Proverb. I want his Black body to grow up. I want him to learn to run like his daddy . . . maybe learn to paint . . . play drums . . . be nerdy, lanky, learn to jump. But I know he will also see dead Black bodies. He will have questions. And I don't know if I will have answers. What I do know: *Black people deserve love. Black people don't deserve bullets. Black people deserve tenderness. Black people don't deserve terror.*

I know that one day he will nestle in my arms, and we'll cry together. My poor child and I will cry, because we will know the terror *together.* We will both have to try to find our song to sing. We will both have to strain our necks forward hoping to produce a faint note, a whisper, strong enough to keep us going. When that happens, because I know it will, I will anoint his head with the oil of my Black prayers that came from my mother's Black lips over my Black body as she quoted Black people's most cherished verse: "Yea, though I walk through the valley of the shadow of death, I will fear no evil; for thou art with me; thy rod and thy staff cover me." I will let him know what she let me know: *Jesus does not forget Black bodies. Our Black bodies.*

Jesus does not forget bruised and abused Black bodies. That is good news. But I know that this word will not always be enough because my son and I will have to enter back into a world that does not protect bodies like ours. Now I understand what my momma and my daddy were trying to teach me about entering back into a country that believes our bodies to be dangerous bodies. Our living will have to be our revolt, as Frantz Fanon writes, because we can no longer breathe in this country that has its foot on our necks.

I know that I will have to teach him something else I had to learn: Don't ever get used to this. Don't you ever get used to this.

RAGE.

But a bird that stalks
down his narrow cage
can seldom see through
his bars of rage
—MAYA ANGELOU, "CAGED BIRD"

"**W**hat radicalized you?" was the question that ran across my news feed. I saw that question, took a long pause. I tried to think back over the past few years of my life, thinking about my journey with Jesus, thinking about all the ways I learned to run, thinking about all the ways I was trying to figure out life, all the dead Black bodies I had seen, all the James Baldwin books I had read, *Notes of a Native Son, Nobody Knows My Name, The Fire Next Time, The Cross of Redemption.* So I quickly quote-tweeted two names: "JESUS & JAMES BALDWIN."

I thought about the ways both Baldwin and Jesus shaped how I thought about myself, my Black body, my world, this country. When I wrote it, my mind replayed passages I'd read of each, their profound concern for love and liberation, the way they stood with those who felt unseen, unheard, marginalized, and left out. Both meant so much to me and gave my life such deep meaning.

Only thing is: That was a lie.

It wasn't Jesus nor James Baldwin who radicalized me.

It was white people.

Apathetic white people.

THE CHURCH WE WERE AT SAID THEY WANTED TO BE A more *diverse* church. That they wanted to accomplish *racial reconciliation*. After the Trayvon Martin murder, white Christians slowly began to host "conversations" about ways they could bring people together.

Our church was no different. It seemed that after every high-profile event of a Black body being murdered or terrorized, they joined in a chorus of white Christians who wanted to use our voices and bodies not so much to free them both, but to make themselves look better than they actually were. Somehow white people always wanted to make statements and public proclamations of their own progress while using our faces.

After the 2016 presidential election, and the rifts that the church began to feel, the leaders picked me to take a small group through a book on race. I was excited to finally have a dedicated space at church where we could finally talk about the violence that was happening in our world.

I come to find out that this "book on race" was written by a white pastor, John Piper. My church had chosen his book because, as many of them said, he "presented a biblical view on race." Before that moment, I had not read a book on race, or one that talked about Christianity and race. The leaders talked about how good of a job Piper did and how helpful the book had been. Looking back on it now, having read the book, it confuses me that the same people who decried so many of us talking about race didn't mind hearing about race from a white man who ironically admitted his own racism and failures, and who had curious ways of evading discussion of white supremacy while talking about racism.

All of the members of my group were white, but not all of them were the same. I had both what my grandparents called *very nice white Christians* and what Kiese Laymon calls *the worst of white folks.* We had gathered at the home of one of the members. As each member brought in their food for the night, we greeted each other, asked how the day had gone, and talked about what we thought the night's meeting would be like. Before the meeting began, we said a prayer and talked over our plan for tackling the book. Some were excited. Some were indifferent. Some were like one of the members, an old white man, who said, "I'm just coming to the meeting to see what you [the young Black man] had to say." He really didn't want to see or understand, but would rather, as I would find out later, talk about the latest conspiracy he'd heard on conservative talk radio.

I also had those who actually wanted to see some change, who really wanted to learn the language and way of racial justice, which for a moment made me optimistic. But for every earnest, genuine, curious white person present, there was also the kind that joined the group to argue with me week in and week out. Why Thomas Sowell was right. Why they needed me to listen to their "divine" revelations about the problems of Black life. And their favorite phrase, "Black men needed to stop killing Black men."

The group was both an experience and a head-ache. The thing is, in my group and in the church, those who didn't want anything to change outnum-bered those who did. The leaders didn't think so, they didn't think many in the church didn't want to see change, but I knew, even if I didn't say much.

Then things began to get bad. Real bad.

Instead of a humble spirit and an openness to

learn, many became hostile in ways that were becoming too much to bear. I met with the leaders to no avail; they always preached to me a message of "have grace and patience" with them. I knew what they meant but that was too much to ask of me. They were not there. They didn't feel what I had felt. They believed the best about the white people they had so much history with. I started to ask questions about this country, the Christianity baptized in whiteness I was surrounded by, the rhetoric of responsibility devoid of justice, the apathy, the "Jesus didn't come to change society."

I was confused by so many of the responses. Before I knew what a microaggression was, I knew what they were saying was exhausting. They didn't say anything good about Black people but always spoke of us in ways that made it seem that we were less moral, less intelligent, and more dysfunctional. It was so exhausting. The more I read Piper's book, the less I became convinced of it. The less I became convinced of his confidence and ability to save white people. The less I became convinced of the Black people—the conservative Black people—that he so loved to quote. The less I became convinced that the "gospel," as so many had said, would make white people less racist. I found myself doing more than trying to persuade white people about the society that we lived in and the ways I was learning to talk about it. It was existential—I was trying to prove to them that we were human, that we loved this country, but this country didn't love us back. It was like, Cathy Park Hong writes, explaining to a person why you exist, or why you feel pain, or why your reality is distinct from their reality. Only problem is, in their mind, our reality didn't exist.

"Haven't we made so much progress in this country?" one member said.

"If the depictions look Arab, wouldn't Christ look like a terrorist?" another said. And it just kept coming.

"Are there any Blacks addressing helping others actually get skills? Are they addressing fatherlessness?"

"Yeah, I had the realization that I have to accept I'll be submitting to a Black man," another member told me over the phone.

"There is an anti-intellectualism in the culture . . . and it's especially true in the Black church."

"I have Black friends."

"All lives matter."

"It's a sin problem, not a skin problem."

They just kept coming. I was so confused. In my mind I'm just wondering: *How could they be around us Black people and say that? How did they not know us? Why aren't the leaders speaking up about this?* I was just so, so confused. But my confusion was turning, turning into something that I could no longer ignore or hide or run from or lie about. I could no longer act like everything was just aite.

.   .   .

I HAD STARTED THINKING MORE DEEPLY ABOUT MY Black body, the white church, white apathy, and the white hostility I was experiencing. There was a war going on inside of myself. I had questions and I didn't know where to get the answers. Ironically, though, I still was optimistic about the goodness of white people and their ability to love us. I was still optimistic that the gospel that I heard as a young kid was the same gospel that would free them from their delusion. I went to church. I went home. I read books. I worked out. I went to work and was in the normal swing of things, renting cars, cleaning cars, running cars to the airport, taking breaks, renting cars, cleaning cars again.

"Yo, what y'all think about the election?" I asked my co-workers the morning after the group I was leading met. Mikayla, someone who reminded me of Angela Davis, started to go off. There was pain in the room. All of my co-workers were Black. It was like a therapy session. But then I added, "Now, we still need to be concerned about racial reconciliation. White people are changing." I said this with a dumb confidence. Mikayla looked at me. She gave me that crooked look like something was missing, or wrong, or ignorant. Her mouth twisted and turned as she cocked her head to the side. "Stew, these white people over and over again have chosen white supremacy over us," she said. "I don't care if you preach in their churches, I don't care if you are around them, I don't care how many Black people are around, I don't care how nice they are, they have been socialized to see you as less than." I started to get uneasy as I dismissed her as being too radical, too angry in my mind. I was performing the sexist lie that Black women need to stay silent, that I as a Black man was always right.

"Now, Mikayla," I responded, "I was the first Black person to preach at this church . . . they definitely want to see me as equal."

We went back and forth, back and forth. The other co-workers looked at me, some laughing, some giving me the same twisted look Mikayla did.

Eventually, Stew the Church Boy came out.

"Until Black lives matter to us, it won't matter to them," I said.

"Nooo," everyone began to shout.

Mikayla then looked at me and said words that I'll never forget: "Stew, you don't have a damn thing to offer Black people. A damn thing."

I was stunned. No one had ever told me that before. She walked out of the office as we were shutting down for the day. I was part enraged, part confused, part sad. I didn't say anything to anyone. I walked out and headed home. I pulled up to the house, taking off my tie as I walked in the door, smelling like car cleaner and air freshener from the cars I had rented out that day. I begin to tell my wife what happened.

"Baby," I tell her, "you won't believe what Mikayla told me today." She had gotten used to my complaining sessions after a day at Enterprise.

"What?"

I angrily told her about how Mikayla had treated me. How it made me feel, how upset I was. Jasmine gave that *You on your own, playa* sigh.

"You always listening to other people when I've been telling you this the whole time."

A dagger. I felt so much shame, so much. I felt like I had let so many people down, but more than that, in the moment, I knew I had let my wife down. I didn't listen to her. I was oblivious. It was as if all the shame of just how much I'd distanced myself from my Blackness, and how much white people mattered more than my wife, and how much I'd failed at being the husband that she needed, and how I lacked the honesty needed to face myself, and how terrible I had become had hit me like a flood. The lack of feeling deeply the tragedy of Mike Brown and the Charleston church massacre. The lengths I went to prove myself and to assimilate to whiteness. The lack of support I got. The things I put my wife through just to be in ministry.

"Baby," I told her, "I'm sorry. I never should have put you through any of this." I knew I had nothing to say to her that would make things right or heal the pain. I knew that nothing I would say would change the terrible ways I had learned to love her. All I could do was tell her, "I'm sorry."

Later that night, I walked out of the house to sit in my truck.

There I wept. I felt so powerless, so vulnerable. I hated myself in that moment. So much within me wanted to run. But more of me needed to tell Jas how much I wanted to change how cold I had been. I had bargained with myself and white people to prove my worth, to prove over and over again that I belonged, that I was worthy of their praise and my position. But Jas had shown me a mirror of myself, and I hated what I had become.

It was painful, it was a flood, I was enveloped. I wasn't in denial anymore. I just hadn't learned how to love myself or my wife as much as I loved proving myself and praise.

I told myself over and over again that I would never become that terrible again. I didn't hate my body. I hated my insides. I didn't hate myself the same way I tried to love white people. I had to admit I was depressed. I knew I needed to change. No amount of theology I read, no amount of songs I sang, no amount of prayers I prayed, seemed powerful enough to change how I was feeling.

How could I not see it?

How have I been so blind?

What has this made me?

Weeks later, I was leaving the church after Sunday service. It'd been another long, lonely morning. My friend Drew Hall stopped me and told me he'd noticed the changes that I had started making over Facebook posts and in conversations he was having with me. Drew was white, tall, and had a love for smoking meat and lamenting about Georgia Tech sports. Ironically, Drew, being a white brother, told me he had a book that he felt I needed to read. I agreed to read it. He met me after church and handed me Martin Luther King, Jr.'s *Where Do We Go from Here: Chaos or Community?*

The purple and gold colors, Martin's powerful preaching voice: Drew didn't know it at the time, but this was the first book I read written by a Black person. I didn't want to admit to him, nor others, that I hadn't read much about what I'd been angry about. I knew what I felt, but I didn't know how to put words to my wounds.

When I arrived home that day, Jas was sitting in the living room, watching one of her latest shows. She hadn't gone to church that day. She had resolved not to go anymore. I walked upstairs and into my office, and sat at my table. I pulled out the book and began to read. I read for hours. I read and read and read. I couldn't put it down. I lost track of time. I grabbed my pen and began underlining as much as I could. It was as if Martin had showed up in my room. This was a different Martin than the one the white Christians around me quoted about judging others by the content of their character. This was a different Martin from the terrible ways they talked about his

Christianity, and how he had been a Marxist, and that he didn't believe like they believed, and that he wasn't as important as we had thought. It was like reading the gospels; I felt the power of Jesus, the news of the liberation of the oppressed. I read through King's critique of white people, their lack of reeducation out of their racial ignorance, their myths of America as a Christian nation, their commitment to white supremacy. I read through his thoughts on Black Power, both his critique and praise, his radical imagination of Black politics and the fierce urgency of liberation. I had gotten used to the people I was around sanitizing King, making him the prophet of white gradualism and colorblind Christianity.

Then he quoted James Baldwin. In "A Letter to My Nephew," James Baldwin wrote: "Please try to remember that what they believe, as well as what they do and cause you to endure, does not testify to your inferiority, but to their inhumanity and fear."

I felt afraid and tired. I had always been afraid of what other people thought of me, what they would do to me, what they would make me. But now, I was more afraid of what I had become.

Baldwin's words hit me with a sort of mercy, a grace, as if almighty God was speaking, reaching down to touch my wounded flesh with his words: "You don't be afraid. I said it was intended that you should perish . . ."

It was then that my dungeon shook, the foundations of my soul rumbling under the thunderous roar of each syllable. The chains, one by one, link by link, fell off. I was not afraid. I was not afraid anymore.

Preachers I grew up with always loved to talk about Ezekiel and the dry bones. They became like prophets, talking to God, wondering if bones could live. Bones bruised by white supremacy, bones lynched, bones broken through policy, bones shattered through pain, Black bones. So they prophesied to those bones, weak though they were; the bones began to rumble, rumble, shake, rumble, shake. The sinews and the flesh began to come to life. It was fire, burning, blazing, fire shut up in those bones. They came back to life; they rose again. I came back to life.

My tears had stopped. They had been wiped away. They turned to rage.

I WAS DONE TALKING ABOUT UNITY. I WAS DONE TALKING about coming together. I was done with it all. It was time to talk about white supremacy.

After I'd finished reading King and Baldwin, I started to speak up differently about things I was seeing both in my church and in the country. People didn't believe me, but that didn't scare me anymore. This time, I knew what I was talking about. I had the voices of the ancestors with me.

For so long, something in me made me believe I could save the worst of whiteness. From a very early age we are baptized in messages of unity and good-ness, believing in the gospel of American progress. So I tried that. For years and years I tried—from the white worship nights at Clemson to the Georgia church that once felt like home and soon revealed itself to be anything but. I was driven not by Jesus's gospel, but by an American myth: that the descen-dants of slaveholders and segregationists would put down their swords of pride, surrender their need for supremacy, and finally love us.

"Race and religion, it has been remarked," Bald-win writes, "are fearfully entangled in the guts of this nation, so profoundly that to speak of the one is to conjure up the other." As Baldwin encountered the major shifts in religion and politics of the 1980s, he saw just how deeply intertwined history, identity, and politics were. As both the nation and the churches in the nation tried to grapple with the enduring prob-lem of white supremacy and the ongoing battle to imagine a better America, Baldwin grappled with the tragic dimensions of Black life as it experienced white hatred: hatred from white Christians and white America. White America and evangelical Christians were always trying to save people and keep the coun-try white. This led Baldwin to declare that he "can-not take seriously—at least, as Christian ministers—the present-day gang that calls itself the Moral Major-ity." This gang, a sort of mob, had "taken the man from Galilee hostage."

I knew I couldn't just use the best of my work for them. Too many of us were dying; way too many more were traumatized. I needed to give voice to God's action in the Black experience, our suffering, and our resistance. I needed to bear witness to the struggle for our freedom. I needed to give voice to being fully Black and fully Christian.

The Jesus I preached must make us *free,* not quiet. Not just Christian but Black. I needed to be around other Black folk who knew about the apathy of white folk to dead Black bodies. Who knew about anointing oil, midnight tarrying services, pig feet and livers with hot sauce, praise breaks and protest, because the people around me didn't see or know me, see or know us. I needed to be around folk who knew that Jesus was a penniless preacher from the poor side of Nazareth. I needed to be around folk, like my grandmama and granddaddy, who prayed and faced down empires but still were living. I needed, as Toni Morrison writes, to grow up Black again.

AROUND THAT TIME, I WAS READING THE BOOK OF NEhemiah. For the first time in my life, I realized that someone in the Bible was angry. My Christianity up until that point had neither room nor language to talk about the ways rage could be a fuel for love and a balm for healing. Christians were not to be angry or enraged at the terrible things going on around us.

Christians were meant to just love, and that love never meant marching in the streets, testifying in the halls of Congress, preaching audacious messages of liberation from pulpits. Calls for unity were an excuse for silence in the face of Christian complicity in abuse, injustice, and disrespect. Jesus had been weaponized to keep us silent about white supremacy and anti-Blackness. That Jesus, I had to get rid of him. The sanitized version of Nehemiah's story, where the rage that he spoke of was seen more as a misunderstanding than a spiritual necessity, I had to get rid of. I started to read his story as my story, my story as his story. The people in the Bible were not just distant figures. They were those who knew the struggle of oppression, fighting for your personhood, and the ever-complex relationship with God in the midst of struggle. I, like James Cone, began to read the Bible through the lens of Black power, Black arts, and the Black consciousness movement. Nehemiah for me had become not just a gifted spiritual leader but a revolutionary. He had become my Fred Hampton. I pulled out my journal, grabbed my gel pen, and wrote: "Nehemiah's rage set them free."

I knew mine would as well. I knew Black rage was a pathway to hope and liberation. I couldn't just write about ministry anymore and just preach about hope and act as if this country wasn't burning and we weren't being consumed in the fire that white supremacy created. My rage meant giving up convinc-

ing white people to see that I was a human and
worthy of love and worthy of being seen and worthy
of being protected. My rage meant loving us, and
really loving Black people, by giving us something
meaningful for our freedom and our future and remembering our pain and giving voice to our ancestors. Black Lives Matter was not just an affirmation of
our dignity in the face of white apathy and white
hatred. Black Lives Matter became gospel to me,
good news in a world that forgot us, abused us, and
terrorized us with impunity. Rage is a powerful political emotion, writes Audre Lorde. One that, with
clarity, can become "a powerful source of energy
serving progress and change."

After running from rage my whole life, it took
some getting used to. I noticed that rage neither set
me free nor made me feel better. But it did give me
some words and some energy to fight white supremacy in myself and white supremacy in the world, and
all the ways white supremacy destroyed us and those
we loved. It shook me out of my illusion that the
world as I now knew it was the world that God
wanted. It forced me to deal with the ways in which
my Black body and Black children, women, and men
live in a system of injustice—a system of inequality,
exploitation, and disrespect. It became my public
outcry that our bodies and our souls must be loved,
and that our bodies and our souls mattered to God,
and that our bodies and our souls must find rest.

I started to see that my Black rage in an anti-Black world was a spiritual virtue.

As I read the scriptures and the history of our people, I saw rage not as just a good idea but the right of a people who have had their bodies devalued, abused, and oppressed. It is constant and it is conscious. Black rage is the work of love that protests an unloving world. It is the good news that though our society has often forgotten us, there is Someone who loves us and believes us worth fighting for. Those who were more concerned with the responses of my Black rage than they were about a system that justified our Black death didn't love Black people—they loved when we stayed in our place. And that's not love, that's hate.

Black rage is tricky in America. It has, as Mychal Denzel Smith writes, been used against us. We have been told that to affirm one's Blackness and to be enraged means we hate white people—even when we're enraged by *the worst of white folks.* So many have wrongly dismissed our Blackness, our criticism of white supremacy, and our rage—our fight for our future and our dignity—as unloving and unnecessary. When we ourselves do this, we dismiss the legitimacy and genius of our Black tradition—the literary genius of Toni Morrison, the prophetic fire of James Cone, the radical vision of Martin and Malcolm, the political savvy of Frederick Douglass, the deep love of bell hooks and Baldwin. All of these greats, from Ida

B. Wells to Fannie Lou Hamer, from Richard Allen to Fred Hampton, from Angela Davis to Black Lives Matter, from Frantz Fanon to Katie Cannon, all these were motivated by deep love, and all these were enraged at the system of white supremacy. Rage became their gospel—their good news in a country that believed we should not be outraged, but silent. So they picked up their pens, mightier than a sword, and they slashed through the flesh of American innocence, allowing itself to see the blood on its hands, and the blood in its streets, and the blood in its schools, and the blood in its churches, as people pledged allegiance to it more than they did to love, to justice, and to caring for other Americans.

One of the things about Black rage that scares people is that our minds understand rage, but mostly what Carol Anderson calls white rage. See, the difference between Black rage and white rage is that white rage is rooted in violent control of land and people, and a backlash to Black progress, Black citizenship, and Black folk simply being able to drive where they want, play where they want, love how they want, and live how they want. Black rage, in many ways rooted in a certain narration of Moses, the Prophets, and Jesus, is rooted in a quest for Black dignity, self-determination, safety, power, and a democratic and liberated future for all people. It is a people's audacity to fight for Black life and love. To affirm one's personhood, to affirm one's Blackness, in a society that terrorizes both the individual and the community, is to affirm that our lives matter to God and should matter in our society. It is a push against systems of dominance that assault the Black body and soul. White rage, which we have known all too well, has been a way of rolling back civil rights, voting rights, human rights for Black people in America and across the globe. It has opposed any aspect of progress, not just for Black people, but for any who are forgotten in society. One of the big differences is how Black rage and white rage imagine and envision the future. White rage imagines a future where white supremacy rules. And it has killed for it. Our rage envisions a future where all people are free, loved, and worth something. And we have died for it.

Rage, I began to see, is complex. For we are more than my rage, more than what white supremacy has done to me.

I began to see that being enraged becomes dangerous when it is not channeled through love, serious deep love for ourselves and our neighbor. It can become a lonely place, and I have had my struggle with loneliness. When rage becomes the spark that embraces Black flesh, moves us to universal love, to struggle, to fight, to pray, to embrace, to remember, this becomes a sword and shield. In a world that wounds our souls and bodies, this becomes the work of love: holy, healing, and liberating work. Love dancing with rage, rage dancing with love, becomes the greatest spiritual, moral, and political task in each generation. It is a call for us as Black people to what Jesus called abundant life, spirit of the Lord upon Black flesh, freedom for all people.

When I stopped running from the pain, rage showed up. And it taught me to seek freedom.

Rage revealed to me its cousin, courage, and the ways we need both for liberation. The courage to leave. The courage to refuse to believe what white people have said about me or have done to me. The courage to stare down white supremacy and be Black, love being Black, to fight for Black people.

Rage liberated me from my lies and gave me the courage to see anew the present and the future.

I knew that rage could not protect me, or my wife, or my son, or any of the Black folk I loved and cared deeply for. I knew that rage would not set us free in the ways our Black mommas and Black daddies spoke of. I knew that rage would not bring any of our dead back to life. But I knew that rage would make me rise again.

Rage has a way of making us stand up. Of freeing us from fear. Rage made me stop running, and it made me stop lying.

Soon, rage would put my faith back together in all the ways it was shattered.

BACK ROADS.

We are things of dry hours and the invol-
  untary plan . . .
And yesterday's garbage ripening in the
  hall,
Flutter, or sing an aria down these rooms
    —GWENDOLYN BROOKS, "KITCHENETTE
      BUILDING"

was one of those kids who loved preachers.
Toward the end of service, when the sermon
was on the way to its crescendo—what I later
would learn is called the *whoop*—I would imitate
him (for they were always male). I would grab
the Martin Luther King, Jr., fan my mom would
have sitting beside us, rip off Martin's precious,
stern, bold face, and throw my hand on my hip.
My little body, my oversized jacket, my mind
picturing crowds of deep, dark faces: I whooped,
and I whooped, and I whooped. I was preach-

ing. Then in a flash, as if caught up in some sort of mysticism, the other members around me shouting, the musicians following the preacher's cadence, my little body would let loose, I would run, I would shout. There I was, young, Black, free. Maybe that was the meaning. Maybe that was where I found, beneath it all, a deep love for justice, Blackness, liberation.

Though I felt free, I also felt the ways the church would restrict us. We could dance, but never too much. We could sing, but never out of order. We could run, but never like grown-ups could because, in their mind, we were "playing" church. They thought that we were playing with God, never taking seriously that God was as close and as real as the rain and the dark skies that we could see outside the church windows. They took themselves and God seriously. They just never really took us as children seriously, or the ways we learned how to be free seriously, or the ways we had learned how to call on Jesus just like they did. We were never really good at listening to them, but over time, and in many ways, we were always good at imitating them. We imitated their contradiction: a faith that loves to leap and dance and a faith that fails to take others seriously. I couldn't really understand why the grown-ups in the church were so hard on us.

My mother and father, one a faithful sister and the other a faithful deacon, would have us in church all day. Sundays were like this. I would get up, try to sneak an NCAA game in on the PS2, then I'd hear my momma cooking breakfast. Really I would smell it. The smell of smoked sausage, scrambled eggs baptized in butter, grits, and biscuits. Our house wasn't that big; smells and sounds traveled easily. Faintly in the background I would hear Bobby Jones's high-pitched laugh on BET as my mother, as she would say, got her heart ready for service. The next video would come on, "Mary Mary," as she let out a deep hum following the lyrics about shackles being broken. The next, Kirk Franklin. The next, Fred Hammond. We would get dressed in our Sunday's finest. Though I wouldn't let her know, I hated wearing suits. Like hated, hated it. But she was my momma, and I really had no choice in it. It wasn't a hill worth getting a beating over.

My dad would grab his old washboard, the one that became his personal instrument at church, the kind that old Black folk would use to wash their clothes on. They would scrub away the smell of old chicken guts. They would scrub away the stains of dark oil. They would scrub away the musk. They would scrub away the "outside." Dressed in his black suit with his bold black tie, he made it clear: This day is different. Then he would grab the metal hanger, his thick rough hands slowly removing it from the cardboard coating, put it in a figure eight, throw it in the back of the van, and we would head to church in our green Ford Windstar. This was his way of going to church. This was his way of doing ministry. Sounds of metal clanging like cymbals and sounding like a bunch of nothing. This was his way of teaching me that no matter what, when Black folks' hands touch the things of this world, they could take something that would smell like chicken guts on Wednesday and turn it into something that made bodies shake on Sunday. I never really asked him why he played the washboard and didn't take up a real instrument like I did with the drums, Dominique with the guitar, and Dion with the bass. That was a part of him I could tell he cherished, but I never really found a way in. The way he put it under his armpits, the way I would watch him close his eyes, cocking his head to the side, his left hand holding the washboard, and his right hand going up and down, up and down. He loved it and he held it close, as close as he held us when he hugged us.

The church folk wouldn't really let us play the instruments during praise and worship until, according to Bishop Morris, who was the pastor, we were "filled with the Holy Ghost with the evidence of speaking in tongues." (Yeah, that long.)

Bishop was an old working-class Black southern pastor who had a bald head. He was short, brown, slim, and walked with the slowness of someone who has been through something. Whenever I would walk into his office, I would look around and see all the pictures of his children, of the awards he had won, and, most of all, of his military service. He never talked about his service to the country. He would always talk about Jesus and how we needed to act right so that one day, when the grades were called during Young People's service, we could be awarded one whole dollar bill. I think his service in the military made him both disciplined and strict. He would always catch us after church, either handing us some candy, teaching us a new lesson about how to handle ourselves in the white schools we were going to, or even handing us another dollar just because he knew that would be a way of telling us that he loved us. He did all these things, but made sure that we never played the instruments unless we were really saved. We could only play them after the service, or when one of us asked for the keys to the church so that we could play on Saturdays or early before Sunday service.

I always thought that to be too confining, too constricting to what we could possibly become. Even though we played church in the living room, around the dinner table, in the car, turning pencils into microphones and notebooks into tambourines, when we were in the sanctuary, it was the *real* thing, they said. The place was sacred. There was no playing, no running, no joking. Maybe that was their way of saying that when you deal with God, it's no laughing matter. God didn't really joke or laugh with us. I always thought them acting this way toward us ruined the fun of cutting up with my cousins and friends, skipping out on church and running to the gas station to grab a chicken tender plate. Potato wedges. Hot sauce. Honey mustard. Orange Fanta. Heaven.

Though Bishop and the leaders of the church didn't let us play too much, they did try to love us, to teach us. The sermons that we heard were part poetic oration, part folk wisdom, part celebration. Each was meant to move our bodies and our hearts. Each was meant to make us burn with fire—the fire of the Holy Ghost, that is. We were meant to burn, like lamps in dark places, with our dark faces and beautiful bodies. The messages that we received were that our bodies mattered. Many of the saints—that was the dignifying language used—had survived in a country that had not loved them back. For the moments they had, they wanted to really love us. They wanted to instill in us a faith that was as Black as it was beautiful, as real as it was mythical. The language of faith that they used was language through tongues, bodies moving to and fro. Drumming and skillful walking up and down the Hammond organ. Faith was not a message; it was a movement, of body, of mind, of soul, of spirit. It was an audacious adventure. It was courage in the face of the absurd, yet as honest and as human as sitting patient, waiting on the coming of the Lord.

My momma is what people would call a singing

woman. People loved hearing her sing songs in church. I did, too. It was good to say, "That's my momma," as she would go into her trance, the whole church going into an uproar. She was also a praying woman. I was afraid of her prayers as a kid. At times I would be awakened in the middle of the night to footsteps, pacing up and down our small hallway. I would go to the bathroom, wiping my eyes, trying to orient myself, and hear her. Off in the living room she had stopped to get on her knees. She would be praying. It was quiet, real quiet. But I could hear her tongues. Then I could hear our names. "Lord, protect my children," she would say. "Lord, open up my children's minds," she said. "Lord, let them know that they are loved," she said. "Lord, I'm tired," she said. "I'm so tired." One by one. She prayed over us. She prayed like she was afraid. She loved us but she also wanted to protect us, she wanted to *cover* us.

My siblings and I used to think this was crazy. Hearing your momma pray over you, crying and in tears. Begging God to keep you. Was she afraid of God? Was she afraid that somehow God would punish her if she didn't pray enough? Or if bad things happened it would be her fault? Should we be praying like that? I don't know. I just know she prayed and she prayed. Prayer, I learned, was her place to deal with her pain. It was the sacred space between her Black body and God. And she could say whatever she wanted. She could cry. She could argue. I never heard her curse, she wasn't like that, though I'm sure there was time she wanted to. Prayer was one of her last defenses in a world she knew didn't care about her body, our bodies, her prayers, or our protection.

THE THIRD DEAD BLACK BODY I SAW WAS PHILANDO. July 6, 2016. The day after Alton Sterling died, everybody saw Philando Castile on their screens. He in his white shirt, covered in bloodstains as police officer Jeronimo Yanez snatched his beautiful soul from him. All over social media his Black body traveled. Yanez had stopped Philando for a brake light being out. A brake light. How many other cars had he passed? How many? I will never know. We do know one he didn't and that one, with Philando, his girlfriend, and his baby girl sitting in the back seat, ended in murder. We didn't know this until the dashcam video came out, but I counted seven shots.

Bang. Bang. Bang. Bang. Bang. Bang. Bang.

His girlfriend in a fearful panic cries, "Nooooo." I could tell that Diamond Reynolds couldn't believe what she was seeing. Who could? She did the best thing she knew how: record. What a tragedy. The only thing she could do in that moment was open the Facebook app, go live, and hope someone else saw the horror that she was seeing. So she filmed.

"You just killed my boyfriend," Diamond screams

out. Philando is crying out in pain. His last gasp in terror shakes me to my core. This is not just crying. This is pain. Crying out in real pain like we did as kids. Pain that reaches deep down in your bones. Pain that burns. Pain that severs. "I wasn't reaching." Officer Yanez didn't care about that. He screams at him again, after he shot him, "Don't pull it out!" He had shot him seven times and he was still making commands.

"He wasn't."

"Don't move!" Philando is not moving. The hot metal has already entered his dark flesh.

"Get the baby girl out of here."

"Oh noooooo," Diamond yells.

I hear Philando panting. His breath. Heavy. Weak. Patterned. Still weak. He gasps in and out. The gun is still pointed at his wounded flesh. He is dying. A slow death. In front of millions of people who can do nothing. He pants and gasps for air. I hear Diamond frantic and crying. She by some force has been able to hold the phone steady to tell Philando's story. We all knew that without footage, our stories would not be believed, and even with footage, we would be blamed. Philando was. "Stay with me," she tells Philando as the video pans from her distressed face, Yanez's black gun pointed at Philando's dying body. "Please, Jesus, don't tell me my boyfriend went out like that," she says. They tell her to exit the car. She asks for her daughter who just heard the sounds of loud gunshots, close enough to make your eardrums go numb for hours. She exits. Philando is dying.

They pull his body from his white car, in his white shirt, covered in blood, still warm, not moving. Philando is dead. He died in front of his girlfriend, his daughter, and millions of us who saw it. Three million. She had no one else to call. No higher authorities. The police had shot him, over a brake light, as he reached for his wallet that the officer had asked for. We all saw it and it burned. She wanted us to see what we already knew: *Philando's body was not saved.* No matter how beautiful we thought he was, no matter how brilliant we knew him to be, how gentle, loving, kind, strong, none of that was able to save his body. None of it.

I was enraged.

Many of the white Christians in my church did not see Philando as I did. I saw a person; they saw a problem. There was always something about Black bodies that must be blamed. Yanez blamed Philando. Other white people I was around blamed Philando. How could they think this about him, I wondered, how could they, once again, blame us for our own deaths? By that time, I was exhausted. Every conversation I entered, I wasn't just arguing for them to see just how poor their views were; I was arguing for both Philando's and my right to live. Arguing with people who said they loved Jesus. Arguing with people who said that they wanted reconciliation. Arguing with people who said they cared about our suffering. Arguing for them to give up their lie that you could say you love us and not fight for us. They didn't believe me. They wouldn't. Neither my tears nor my anger seemed to change them.

I burned with rage as I thought of the myriad ways those around me tried to make me feel that I was crazy about speaking out against the injustices visited upon our Black bodies, and the suffocating nature of white supremacy that we had to live in. I felt that the only way I could make sense of my feelings was to begin to do what so many Black people before me did: write. Writing became a way for me to feel free and a way for me to feel like I wasn't crazy and a way to feel like what I was doing was contributing to the struggle. I knew that I couldn't be out on the streets and I knew that I couldn't change any legislation, but what I could do is give voice to our suffering.

When I first started writing, most of my work was about ministry, about the ways I thought about theology or a John Calvin quote I'd recently read. Then I started to write about racial reconciliation and all the ways Jesus wanted us to be close to one another. Then people who looked like me got murdered. Then I got terrified. Then I started to write more about unity to make me and others feel like we were getting better. Then acts of terror kept happening.

Then I started to write to us and for us, and about us, and really about us in ways that I had learned to write about us from Toni Morrison and James Baldwin. I was terrified, but like Toni had said, this was the time for me as a writer to go to work: when I feel lonely, when I feel pain, when terror suffocates my breath, and when trauma wounds my body. Rage woke me up out of my illusion and writing became my way to love us.

I knew that I didn't have to hate myself, or my people, or our art, or our creativity, or our beauty to be human or to be Christian. My work as a Black, southern, Christian writer meant taking us seriously and not just trying to deconstruct white supremacy and the ways that it wounded us but writing in ways that loved us and healed us and liberated us. Writing became a way of remembering. Remembering became a way of healing. Healing became a way of loving us better, truer, in a way that felt as close as I felt in my heart to Alton, to Philando, and to all of us whose journeys ended before they really got started. To be Black and to be southern and to be Christian and to be a writer meant sitting with James and Toni as the disciples sat with Jesus; listening and latching on to whatever words of comfort and hope and joy we can find in life's contradictions. The way they talked about God and about Black people and about this country opened me up to see that God loves our Blackness so much more than the ways we and others have learned not to love us. They taught me that Jesus loves the Black body deeply and that love was something of pleasure, of maturity, of expectation of growing up and getting better. They were theologians in the truest sense of the word. They wrote of intelligible divine possibilities and offered an alternative world of love beyond the world that white supremacy tried to force us to live in. Theology is not just speaking or wrestling; it is also helping us dream a little bit of the future God has for us.

One of the most damning legacies of white supremacy was not just the way it terrorized us with impunity and devalued us by denying our citizenship and disrespecting us by assaulting our dignity, it was also how it wounded our minds and wounded our souls and wounded our bodies. Any conception of God, Baldwin wrote, must deal honestly with the ways Black people are unloved in American society and in the American church and give us all something that helps us to work for a world in which all bodies experience what God desires. It must break down the walls. It must bind up our wounds. It must restore our joy. It must set us free and make us better—better at loving God, better at loving ourselves, better at creating love in a loveless world.

So the more I read them, the more I let them teach me how to love, the more I learned that my work was about loving us rather than convincing others, the more I got tired of writing to white people about us. I needed to write a word that gave voice to our pain, that didn't diminish it, that didn't let white people steal it from us. I sat with Baldwin and King and Morrison, again and again and again. I thought often about Alton's and Philando's Black bodies and the ways my body was being treated. Many saw us the same: worthless. I read and wrote and tried to find words to help me navigate what I was going through. I needed words. And I found them. "There is no time for despair, no place for self-pity, no need for silence, no room for fear," writes Toni Morrison. We speak. We write. We do language. That is how we heal when our bodies bend and break. That is how the world heals when it is bruised. That is how I healed.

I held my breath. I exhaled. I held my breath again. I exhaled again. I opened up my computer. I began to write.

One year later, the man who murdered Philando Castile was acquitted of second-degree manslaughter and intentional discharge of a firearm.

It's hard to describe the way my body stung; I was already enraged, already knowing deep in my bones the terror that could be visited upon my body. I think for the first time in my life I really felt the bone-chilling loss of faith in this country and in this Christianity that criminalized our dead. I felt what it must have felt like for those who had seen Jesus. The pain. The deep sadness as you saw someone whom you loved be snatched from you. He, too, was murdered publicly. His family and friends watched. His cries, his weeping, the blood flowing from his flesh as he loved those who would not love. I felt what it is like to lose faith, faith in yourself, faith in others, faith in a country to love you back, faith in the right thing being done.

I needed words. And I found them. I needed some way to talk about what I was feeling. And I found them. And they found me. I sat in my study, having just finished dinner with Jas, the smell of curry chicken still on my breath and my clothes. I pulled out my small brown journal, turned the page that had been written on before. July 22, 2017. I wrote four words: *Tears. Anger. Confusion. Scared.* That was where I was. I did not feel hope, faith. I didn't feel all things would be made new. This story was too familiar. Nothing was new about that; it was very old. I had gotten used to hearing stories of people being set free in ways we only could have imagined. So I started to write. I felt that I had to eulogize and honor once again a dead Black body.

In desperation and sadness, trying to find words of faith in the face of Black death, I started to read James Cone. I read *The Cross and the Lynching Tree, The Spirituals and the Blues,* and *Black Theology and Black Power.* I read J. Deotis Roberts's *Liberation and Reconciliation.* I read Stacey Floyd-Thomas's *Deeper Shades of Purple.* I read Black theologians. I read Black historians. I read Black poetry. I listened to Black songs. I looked at Black art. I couldn't find a way out of the dark struggle except by reading Black theology alongside Lamentations and the story of Jesus in the mess of life. It was not so much that Cone had all the answers, but for the first time, I was reading a theologian who looked like me, felt like me, talked like me, loved Jesus like me, who knew the comfort of being around white folk like me, who knew the failures of white folk like me, and who knew he had to leave like me.

I had entered seminary in 2016. I was excited to be learning theology and about church history and preparing myself to become a minister in the white evangelical church we were going to. At one time, I'd called it home. I loved the reading. I had always loved learning and growing and wrestling with others who were still trying to figure things out. By the time I started reading James Cone and others, I knew I had to leave the schools I'd been attending—the Southern Baptist Theological Seminary and the Reformed Theological Seminary. I met great people at both. Brilliant people. But, sadly, the schools, the professors, and the theologians I was studying never really took seriously the life of the Black body in America.

They never really understood the connection between Black bodies being lynched and the body of Jesus being lynched. They never really gave voice to faith in the Black experience, never really took seriously what it might mean for the story of redemption and liberation to find itself coming from Black lips. They never had any need to do that. America worked well for them. Their children were safe. Their theology had nothing to say or to do about the terror of being Black in a world that loved them and killed us. I was far less concerned about what they put on hashtags and the audacious claims of their desire to see people come together than I was about what was happening in their congregations, in their families, in their board meetings, in their schools, and in the ballot box.

If the white folk I worshipped and went to school with and had dinner with had the imagination to see C. S. Lewis's Aslan in *The Lion, the Witch, and the Wardrobe* as Jesus, then I knew there should have been no problem when Black folk said Jesus was Black and Jesus loved Black people and Jesus wanted to see Black people free. Just as they found meaning in the symbol of Aslan's representation of love, I found meaning in the symbol of Jesus's solidarity with Blackness. But, sadly, I found out that many could see the symbol of divine goodness and love in an animal before they could ever see the symbol of divine goodness and love in Blackness.

"I didn't discard European theology," Cone wrote as he reflected on his training and giving voice to Black people's religious experience, "but black theology began with deconstruction—that is, *dismantling*

the oppressive, white theologies I was taught . . . theologies that not only ignored black people but blinded
me to the rich treasure in the black religious tradition."

I felt that. It was not that they didn't have anything to say about Jesus, or that they didn't have anything to say about loving their neighbor, that they
didn't have any room for lament; they did. It was that
the idea of freedom and liberation didn't come from
them, because for them and their children, they were
safe, secure, and loved in a country built for them,
that protected them, and desired their futures as much
as they desired their comfort. They were already free.
It was an abstract principle. Not so for us; Jesus had
to bring his work to us and his struggle for justice for
us. He knew we were somebody and that despite the
failures of the churches we grew up in, they gave us a
space to hear God loves us.

I read Cone and other Black theologians and it
was, to use the word we learned in school, a revelation. Faith did start not in the books and words of
those long gone—it started at the place of the Black
body, a place both of divine and destructive revelation. The Black body revealed both the wages of sin
all around us, as Baldwin writes, but it also revealed
the terrible beauty of those who had loved themselves enough to survive. They were John on the
lonely isle of Patmos writing to us Black folk, giving
us a message of good news in a world that often for-

gets us. For the first time, I had encountered a faith that was ours. I saw why they insisted on saying Jesus was Black. Of course they were not talking about his skin color, though he definitely wasn't white; they were talking about his experience, about his solidarity with the oppressed, about his universal love, about his commitment to God's just future, about his healing of wounds, and his good news that Black life does not end in this moment but will forever be beautiful, worthy, and loved. They knew Jesus knew what it meant to live in an occupied territory, knew what it meant to be from an oppressed people, and in a place that does not care about your religion—at least not the way they practice it—but does care to remind you of its idea about your place in society. The threat that you pose to their lies. They knew Jesus knew what it was like for people who looked like him to care more about being in proximity to those in power, and he knew that those in power did not care about people that looked like him.

I learned to see that there is a connection to the body of Jesus being beat in front of his people in public by authorities, being crucified by the state, and the experience of Black bodies being assaulted and terrorized every day in America. He did not stand with the assaulters but with the abused. Jesus did not stand with state or religious authorities being violent against bodies and marginalizing bodies. Jesus stands as one who knew economic, political, and religious violence but also as one who formed people in the way of resistance, dignity, power, justice, and love.

In the spring of 2018, when Jas and I had finally decided that it was time to leave the church we were attending, I stumbled upon the story of Jesus healing a man in the gospel of Mark. The man is in chains, cut off from his community, caught between threat and danger; his mind is weary, controlled, and destroyed. In this moment, he is suffering in every aspect of his life: spiritual, social, political, psychological, economic, and physical. When Jesus comes to town and confronts the man, he not only sets his mind free but he also breaks his chains, both restoring his dignity and changing the world that he knew most viscerally: a place of terror, dehumanization, and pain. In the gospel, Jesus casts out the evil spirits from the man, sending the spirits into the pigs. The man is free. Jesus restores his dignity, power, agency. But this liberation is not for the man only. This liberation is for the man's community as well. He is not to be free alone. He is not to experience justice alone. He is not to sing and dance alone.

When Jesus casts the demons into the pigs, I wondered: *Why would people choose to be around pigs, rendering themselves ceremonially unclean, cutting themselves off from social, political, and religious life?* The answer is they didn't choose it for themselves. Their oppressors did.

The Romans would want meat when they came to town on their excursions. The pigs didn't just represent uncleanliness. They represented violence toward a people. They represented exploitation, disrespect, and second-class citizenship. No wonder the Romans—and those adjacent to their power—were afraid when Jesus cast the pigs into the sea. They knew what that meant: more loss, more death, more violence. So when Jesus liberates the man, he also intends to liberate the community. He intends to set bodies free from suffering and violence. The man's response of joy and wanting to spread this message of love and liberation is so important. This represents the hopes of oppressed people all over and the hopes of the life of Jesus: freedom to be human, freedom to build life, freedom to love, freedom to work, freedom to create joy.

So when I started seeing the way Black bodies and Jesus's body connect, this is what I found out: When Jesus healed people, he wasn't just concerned about their souls. He was concerned about their bodies. Bodies caught up in oppression and exploitation. Bodies forgotten by the community and the empire. Bodies caught up in the streets. Bodies caught up in school and in cages and in dark lonely rooms that felt like hell on earth. The body in Jerusalem and the body in America were bound together. That is good news in a world that has you bound. That is good news in a world that forgets, that segregates, that terrorizes with impunity. That was the good news of Jesus. That was good enough news for me.

FAITH IS SOMETIMES GIVING UP TO BEGIN AGAIN.

I think a lot about the disciples on the road to Emmaus, those two who had lost faith in a moment of great struggle. I have often heard this story as a story of the triumph of the meeting, then rushing back to Jerusalem to tell the good word. It has been told as a story that moves quickly beyond pain, rushing to have some sort of crescendo of joy. So much of what we hear of Christian stories wanted to move beyond the darkness of Friday night and rush to Sunday, the good news of resurrection on the other side of death, power on the other side of pain. That is indeed part of the story, but there is more. We must look again.

They had been with Jesus; they had seen him. His rugged dark carpenter's hands, making both wood and bodies come alive, dance, shout for joy, become beautiful again. They had also seen those same hands nailed and held to the bloody platform as his dark flesh was broken. They had witnessed poor little children running up to him, nestling in his arms, sharing laughter, probably showing off their little toys, knowing Jesus would have time. They had also witnessed him like a wounded child, helpless, in danger, hurt. Ultimately killed. No, lynched. That's what they witnessed, a lynching.

Now they are on the road. Lonely. Terrified. Maybe one of them threw up from the sickness of witnessing a public execution of a body like theirs. Sort of like we witness them on our cellphones. That churning of the stomach as you see someone pass from life to death. But somehow, by some miraculous force, they keep walking. It may not mean much to us, but witnessing such complex trauma does something to the heart, the psyche. To walk is profoundly courageous.

We know how hard it is to hold out hope when the innocent and nonviolent are met by the empire's sword, its brutal logic of terror and violence unleashed upon those who simply want to live, be free, and build a life for themselves and their children.

As I think about them and us, for we are all the same, it's clear we need to re-imagine the language of faith.

On the road to Emmaus, Jesus appeared. Showing up in a shadow of a memory. He let them feel. They were honest. "We 'had' hope," they say. He gives them a reason to resurrect that hope. It is then that they finally see that they've been speaking to God. It is then that their weary hearts burn with joy.

And then Jesus leaves. After all of that, he leaves.

And they go back, at once to Jerusalem, never the same. They now understood that they needed to lose hope in order to gain it. The hope was not in a theory or in a specific kind of event, but in a person, in the living, in the struggle.

We have known that, and have given up faith in the belief that things will eventually get better, a sort of triumphal note that takes one's mind away from such inhumane violence. Martin Luther King, Jr., lost faith, Fannie Lou Hamer lost faith, John Coltrane lost faith, Malcolm X lost faith, W.E.B. Du Bois lost faith, James Cone lost faith, Ella Baker lost faith, James Baldwin lost faith, Octavia Butler lost faith, Toni Morrison lost faith. My momma lost it. My daddy lost it. But their faith was not a destination; it was a discipline. They had lost faith, but never in themselves, in what could be true of us, and what was true of God, and true in the struggle. I have moved beyond the often triumphal idea of faith as future-only, as progression that doesn't upend power and optimism that does not honestly read history and our present moment, and when I did, faith became life giving and miraculously normal.

Faith is as normal and as powerful as choosing to keep on living in the face of white supremacist capitalist brutality, economic instability, political polarization, religious nationalism, and the ongoing struggle of the distance between faith, Jesus, and our lives in the present. It is as normal as being honest with the world as it is. It is as normal as imagining the world as it can become. It is as normal as the disciples on the road, losing so much, but having the courage to begin again, having the courage to return to the places of terror and violence, with the good news that the world as it is is not the way that it always will be. It is as normal as so many of us screaming that our lives matter, and that our lives will have a future, and that our lives must be free.

I have learned that many of us have not given up on faith, just the way our faith has been used to oppress others. We have not given up on the Bible, just the way it has been used to marginalize others. We have not given up on Jesus, we just know he ain't a blue-eyed white Republican. We're not becoming less spiritual or religious. It's just that we have learned to put up with less, much less. Today many people talk a lot about people leaving churches, giving up on Christianity, and rejecting Jesus. In reality, they have given up on the white supremacist brand of Christianity that cares more about power than Jesus, that does not care enough to take either our bodies or our futures seriously. Like James Baldwin, we are holding on to Jesus while also living with our fear, trauma, doubts, and hope. Our story and the story of Jesus are bound together in faith, hope, love, and community. We are not simply our ancestors' wildest dreams; we are their answered prayers. We are the leaders they prayed for.

We are those who are Black and beautiful, bold and courageous, brilliant and connected. We are pastors, we are activists, we are writers, we are blue-collar workers, we are artists, we are poets, we are teachers, we are politicians, and more. As a preacher and writer, my role is to chronicle the struggle, to give voice to liberation and faith, to make pain and anger known, to keep hope alive, and to join our people in our long walk to freedom—to our vision of a better world.

Faith—honest, deep, vulnerable faith, as Baldwin writes—is about growing up, becoming more loving, more honest, and more vulnerable. It is facing ourselves and what we desire. It is finding a way to begin again each day. It is not that we have the right answer, or all the right solutions. It is that we have found deep meaning in the story of Jesus. We have learned, as James Cone writes, that "being black and Christian could be liberating."

FAITH IS FINDING HOME AGAIN.

When I was growing up, I didn't appreciate the faith that I was being immersed in. Throughout college, I distanced myself from the tongue talking, shouting, dancing and running up the pews, and all the other things I considered embarrassing about being Pentecostal. I never really lost my deep love for our faith, the ways in which it made my body come alive, the ways in which I saw the real connection between faith in Jesus and life in this poor, poor country.

When Jas and I moved back to the South after living in California, my mom would tell me that I needed to come back and visit. You know the ways mommas be like, "Now you know, you need to come back home and see people." I made a practice of visiting family but not really coming back to the church family that shaped me, because we had our own church that we were a part of in Georgia. The church back home loved me for who I was. The church back in Georgia loved me for what I did. The church back home reminded me of freedom. The church in Georgia reminded me of failure. I wanted to go back home but I also didn't want to go back home, because both were confused about what they wanted for me. One wanted me to stay. The other never wanted to let me go.

From time to time, my momma and I would talk about the ways I was happy that Jas and I had made it back to being in church around our people. I told her about the ways Jas felt weird being back, because church was much longer than we had gotten used to. Jas was raised in the Black church like I was, but after college we'd both decided to find a home in white churches. Now, we found home again. I told my momma all about how much I remembered home, how much I wanted to find home, all about the ways they made us stand up during our first time there, to make sure we knew we were home. I told her about all the beautiful faces. All the beautiful music. All the ways my insides shook as praise breaks happened. In my mind I was picturing all the conversations that I was going to have, reliving both the ways I'd hated church as a kid and meaningful stories that helped me understand who I was. It was going to be a good trip.

"Hey, Ma," I said as I told her about my plans to visit church. "How's Bishop doing?"

"He's not doing too well," she told me. I could tell her voice was changing and it wasn't good.

"You need to come back and see Bishop," she said.

"I am."

"When?"

"I'll make a trip in the next few days. Let me see how COVID is going to pan out and I'll come," I told her.

"Okay, make sure you come now."

"Alright. I will. I love you."

"I love you, too, son."

I never got to see Bishop. He died before I got to. When I heard the news, I felt a deep regret. It wasn't just because I didn't get to see him. It was because I didn't get to tell him how much I had appreciated him and loved him for the ways he really tried to love me, by filling my gas up when I came home, by slipping me a few dollars for groceries, by asking about me, by telling my momma and my daddy how proud he was that I had made it out, and that I had made good on the lessons he taught us. He was so proud of me. I was really grateful. I had grown up. I had seen that all they were doing was trying to make do with the best of what they had. I knew what they had gone through, what this country had made them and how they did not believe it. I knew that he tried. And I never got to tell him thank you.

His last memory of me was playing football at Clemson, returning back home over the years, slowly and slowly moving farther away, and never returning again. My last memory of him? Me walking into the church to see his cold, weary, dead Black body, just like my uncle's cold, weary, dead Black body, just like Alton's cold, weary, dead Black body, just like Philando's cold, weary, dead Black body. He had finished his race. Captured in one beautiful life was a story that I saw all around me when I went back home for visitation. When I hugged his family and told them that I was there for them. When I saw all the old saints and their shocked faces as I entered the church, I took off my hat, the reflection of his life playing in the background, me removing my glasses, my tears falling.

I walked up to his body. I put my hand on his hand. I whispered to myself a little prayer. Somehow I needed to honor him and to keep his memory alive in my heart. I needed to show that I had learned, a little too late, but I had learned what it meant to have

Black faith, what it meant to love us deeply. I told him how much I had learned, how much I had seen his faith in the face of such brutality. I had really learned. It was too late, but I had learned. I took my hand off him. I walked out of the door and my grand-mother asked me to take her home. On the way to her house, we started laughing over stories of Bishop, stories of ourselves, stories of this country. We laughed and we laughed. I dropped her off, told her I loved her, and then headed back home. On my way home, I cried, because I knew that was normal, that was the faith. Things impossible can become reality, things oppressive can become just, things unlovable can become new, things dead can become alive. The meaning was in the living, and the moving, and hav-ing our being. The faith was in the laughs, the joy, the dying, the living.

I USED TO THINK TALKING ABOUT BLACK LIFE, OR EVEN Black faith, was about convincing white people to be better. But that's far too limiting. No—I've learned that talking about Blackness is about giving us words; setting our bodies free; living in ways that we feel seen, inspired, protected. It is about deep love, the kind that sees what our ancestors did for us; the kind that enables us to be the kinds of ancestors they were to us.

It is about speaking deeply to our pain and trauma,

but also bringing out our complexity and beauty. After all, we are human. It is not about triumph as much as it is about telling our story, living in and loving our Blackness, being honest. Life is not just fight—it is also love. The way we showed up around the dinner table, in praise breaks and shout tracks, prayer meetings smelling like musk and perfume, the anointing oil pressing my forehead with the sign of the cross, basketball games on dirt courts, Olympics on concrete, livers and hot sauce, choir meeting up at Ryan's after church conventions, being in church all singing songs, learning Bible stories, our heads being grasped by sweaty hands as they prayed for our futures, our bodies being held as tight as newborn babies.

We were not concerned about what white people thought in those moments. We were too busy living, learning to love. Ordinary, hallowed, deep love. We Black boys and Black girls bonded over Black lyrics, notebooks full of love songs to our Black mothers, our Black fathers, our Black sisters, our Black brothers. They were our spirituals. Life and the living was an epistle—a love note.

Black teachers showed Black kids Black Malcolm. Black preachers whooping and hollering about Black Jesus. Black aunties and Black uncles dancing, holding beer and liquor in their Black hands. It was about us. Always about us. All of this told a different story in a white world. We had not believed it; we didn't believe we were *niggers*. We knew us, we knew the beauty. They might not have, but we knew. We had to love our wounded bodies and broken spirits back whole again. Our beautiful and broken, complex and contorted bodies, the myriad of human giftedness, were told: *You are here. You are here to be loved, and to be loved, and to be loved. Very deeply.*

The proof is not in the histories and arguments. No, the proof is our Black bodies, wrapped up in a poetic love song of survival, shouting and dancing and being embraced and being free and being loved. Minds drawing from deep love like Black wells in Black woods in old country rural towns, driving down back roads and talking about dead bishops and alive Black bodies, creating memories and meaning in a country that tried to rip it away from us. Tarrying in the middle of the night calling on Jesus like a friend and savior. Our hearts had become the song for the many babies who cried and cried when their mommas and daddies were taken from them, the unspoken prayer. Putting on our Sunday best, smelling like old perfume, with pink hats and long skirts with stockings in the middle of summer. Trading in oversized suits for work boots and denim outfits just to provide for your family. Finding somehow, in the ugliness of it all, the voices of ancestors crying out to you to live. Black Jesus and Black afros with Black fists in the air becoming good news to Black bodies forgotten in a white world. Crying out from pages of books we never read, songs we never sang, paths we never traveled, marked with beauty and grace, our sacred text becoming our Bibles and our bodies capturing the story of our history and of our crucifixions and of our resurrections. Quoting Bible verses and singing hymns over Kool-Aid, red, purple, blue, fried chicken and green beans—a kingly and queenly feast. Breaking the chains of white supremacy with a body that must be free. All telling you a message that you must never, ever forget: You must find home again. You must find home.

That is faith—evidence of things unknown. Things unheard of. Things unseen. That is faith—the substance of our hope. It was our weary feet and our weary souls and our bruised bodies finding a way to dance and to leap and to rejoice when the world was burning. It is coming out, not smelling like what we been through. Breathing. Panting. Gasping. Alive.

That is faith—living.

WOUND.

> To give ourselves love, to love blackness, is to restore the true meaning of freedom, hope, and the possibility in all our lives. . . . Doing the work of love, we ensure our survival and our triumph over the forces of evil and destruction.
>
> —bell hooks, *SALVATION: BLACK PEOPLE AND LOVE*

There is an old Polaroid of me and my sister, Dominique, that my mom has kept over the years. We were about two or three in this photo. I have on a white shirt, tucked into my green shorts that cover my belly. My sister has bows in her hair, her mouth is wide open; her pink, green, and white floral patterns consume the picture. My mom took it back in the nineties when we were visiting my Uncle Sambo one weekend. In it, my sister is screaming her lungs out as if she saw the fear of her life. I'm sitting on the couch next to her, leaning on her. I am her little brother, but not smaller—I'm chubbier.

I wonder if she looks like that cause she was afraid of Uncle Sambo like I was as a kid. I wasn't afraid of him because he was mean. Nah, he was one of those cool great-uncles that you can't hardly understand. It was because, in my mind, he was always like a Black Gandalf figure. He had some years on him. Old man with a long gray beard. Every time he opened his mouth you could see the teeth missing. He would reach in his left shirt pocket. Pull out the green packet of Ice Breakers. Open the wrapper. Chew. Spit. Chew. Chew some more. Spit some more. I never quite could understand why though. Somehow my sister was crying, probably pulling out her bows like my son does when my wife braids his hair. And there I was, beside her, still. Content.

I think my momma looks at old pictures of us to remind her of joyful moments in life. She hasn't always had those. Her or my daddy. So she, like all the other Black folks we know, keeps cutouts of old newspapers, old *Jet* and *Negro Digest* magazines, obituaries and hymnbooks, comics, and whatever else reminds them of a much simpler time. They have learned to do that. Going back in time allows them to ease some of the stress built up in their shoulders, their backs, their knees, their elbows, their hearts.

My uncle's full name was Samson Jones. He was tall, dark; his skin was oily, smooth. There were cracks in his face that let you know he had been around for years. His hands were rough, the callouses in his palms had become permanent. He, like many Black people during the turbulent years of Jim Crow, escaped from the clutches of the South to head north in hopes of a better future. He wanted to escape American hatred. And he did. He couldn't control the hatred that he left or the hatred that he entered. But what he could control was the terms of his life. He lived the way he did and, in his words, "I didn't give a damn about what white people thought about it." As the spirit of freedom came over Black folk like him in the South, a sort of trance, they gave up on the white man's burden and tried to make a life for themselves up north. They were in search of a better country, tired of dealing with the damning reality of the cold darkness of racial terror. So he left. His family. His life. He left it all behind. He started over.

He settled up in the North pretty well. At least that's what I heard. Like many old Black people, he had his "work" truck, a beat-up white Ford, missing hubcaps and all, that could make it from here to California and back. But he also had his "when it's time to get out" car that he got cleaned, like, four times a week. He was obsessive with this car. When we were kids, we couldn't go nowhere near that car. We could only dream of riding in the silver Cadillac. We stayed in the house, it stayed under the thrice-washed tarp, never revealing quite how much my uncle cared about the car until he removed it. I saw him drive it only maybe once or twice. Black folk in his generation, him being born in the thirties, understood that property in this capitalistic country was a vapor, it could be enjoyed today and gone tomorrow. So you made sure you took care of what you had while you had it.

We would visit Uncle Sambo every time we went up north for a church convention.

LAST YEAR, I GOT A TEXT FROM MY AUNT.

"On Thursday, they are going to check for brain activity." She had mistakenly sent me a message meant for another. I read the rest of the text and was confused. I was confused because I didn't think death, or near death, would come this close to us this year. "If there is none," she said, "they are asking that we withdraw care." I was shook. I had just finished writing a chapter about my uncle and all the ways that he loved us, and all the ways that he survived American hatred, and all the ways I remember traveling from South Carolina all the way up I-95 with my family, and all the ways he laughed, and all the ways the spit from the gum he was chewing would sometimes fall from the cracks of his lips because his teeth were missing. I had just looked at the picture of my sister and me as little children, sitting on his couch, my sister screaming with tears in her eyes, and me beside her, still, calm, my arm across her chest. I had just looked at the picture of all of us visiting him, me in my oversized white shirt and oversized blue jeans and the hat that didn't match either my oversized shirt or my oversized jeans.

We FaceTimed some time ago when my family visited him.

"Heyyy, boy," he said in his raspy voice.

"Sambo," I said.

"It's so good to see you," I said.

"Where's the gum?" I said.

He pulled the pack out of his left shirt pocket, the green mint-flavored gum taking over the center of the screen, his smile widening. "It's right here." I laughed. He laughed. We laughed together.

"If anybody wants me to FaceTime you so you can see him," my aunt said, "and say something to him, let me know." I told her that I did. I knew that I didn't really want to. I didn't really want to face the pieces of him that were left behind, with his heart barely holding on, the same way I barely felt like talking, and the same ways we all barely made it through the year. But I knew that I had to. I had to say something to him.

My phone rang. The grainy video first showed my aunt's face, covered in a mask, her trying to find a way to turn the video around so that I could see Uncle Sambo. She struggled. I laughed a little bit inside because it was the year of our Lord 2020 and she still struggled to flip the camera around. She finally got the camera to turn and I saw him, his body as still as the earth beneath my feet. "Sambo," I called out to him. He did not answer. I wondered if he was dreaming as he was sedated. What goes on in the human mind as it is forced to rest, to be still, to relinquish control of itself and the body that it calls home?

"Hey, Uncle Sambo," I said as I tried to find words for someone who neither hears nor knows that I am calling out to him. "It's good to see you," I said. I lied. It was a lie. It was not good to see him like that. It was not good to see the cracks of his smile shut as the tubes ran down his throat. There was no gum. No missing teeth showing. It was just the digital space between us that allowed me to say some words in what would be his final moments on this side of glory, as the old Pentecostals would say. None of it was good. But I did it because I knew that somehow in the midst of this death-filled year, holding on to what parts of ourselves that still remained, speaking in syllables that carried no weight, reaching down deep inside of ourselves to find some source of sacred belonging, and joy, and peace, becoming gospel to ourselves, these were the stuff of love that would keep our feet moving, our hearts grounded, our palms dry, our stomachs relieved, our minds stilled, our bodies at rest.

So I talked to him even though he didn't respond,

and that was okay because I knew that somehow these words may not have carried the power to raise him, or anyone in rooms next to him, or anyone exhausted from caring for so many suffering people, and all the families welcoming babies into the world and releasing the young and the old alike to the eternal grasp, I knew that these words carried something familiar. They carried me as I had been carried. And it was in the carrying of one another that we believed that we could survive and keep on living beyond the madness.

"Momma wants everyone to go down in prayer at 6:00 in the morning," my aunt texted me. It was 11:42 P.M. when she sent it. I was sound asleep. I didn't dream. I had been too tired. I woke up at 5:34 A.M. I eased my way out of bed and headed downstairs. I opened up my phone and it read: "Hey just letting you know Uncle Sambo passed this morning."

I put my phone down. I took a deep breath. I drank some more water. I started listening to the Spotify playlist that curator Ikechúkwú Onyewuenyi had assembled in hopes of inspiring a new generation of writers. It was the record collection of James Baldwin. Onyewuenyi had said it was a balm of sorts for him. It was the way that Baldwin, as he lived in death-filled years, found a way to speak, and to live, and to love, and to hold on to the pieces of himself and others that tried to flee with each passing moment. "The River Boulevard" by the Pointer Sisters began to play:

And it made me feel so happy!
I didn't know what to say, except:
Thank you! for this life I'm living
And the songs I sing today

I imagined Baldwin hearing those words in the same way and in the same place that I heard them. I imagined him hearing the lyrics and the drum pattern trying to bring his heart rate down as his mind raced with the anxiety of being caught between duty and destruction. I imagine him snapping his fingers, forcing himself to get away from the table and move his legs, and sway side to side, dancing himself into something better. I imagine his tears traveling down his face as his body moved and his mouth cracked a smile as he thought of all the ways he was loved and all the ways he was thankful and all the ways he had been hurt and all the ways he had ran and all the ways he had failed and all the death he had seen and all the ways he had survived. I imagined him too receiving the news of a loved one dying, and facing the heart-wrenching reality of his living, and hearing of all the ways death haunted our bodies and our spirits. I imagined him not wanting to sing, I imagined him as not happy, I imagined him as not saying thank you, I imagined him as looking out of his window, as I have, and seeing the overcast skies, and raindrops falling, and no people in the street. And I imagined him finding a way to dance in it all. I imagined him. I imagined myself. I imagined all the ways we keep on living, and keep on loving, and keep on breathing when we are exhausted, and keep on dancing when our knees are weak, and our stomachs churn, and our minds race between images of black letters on white pages that tell us everything gonna be all right, and bodies motion to our minds that life does not end in this moment. I imagined the trembling in our souls as we are shook. I imagined all that we have lost this year. I imagined all that Baldwin lost. Imagined all that we have. I imagined all of the ways I am thankful.

I imagined it all.

"We have not stopped trembling yet," Baldwin writes, *"but if we had not loved each other, none of us would have survived, and now you must survive because we love you."*

I felt loved. So loved.

I snapped my fingers.

I moved my body.

I danced.

The grief was not over. But Uncle Sambo taught me how to dance amid the trembling.

MY SISTER WAS ONE OF THOSE SISTERS. BECAUSE WE were so close in age, we went through school together until she graduated in 2009. Every single year, we were in school together. I liked it a lot, but sometimes not really. She was like my momma when my momma wasn't around. I couldn't get away with nothing. Absolutely nothing, without somebody threatening to tell my sister. I was the liar. She told the truth. If she said it, I did it, no matter how much I tried to say otherwise.

I called her the other day to check in on her. I do that from time to time. We always talk about old stories together and remind ourselves of things from childhood. We seem to constantly be on a journey of growing up, making sense of things that happen, learning to get better at love. She has a much better memory than I do. So many things that happened in my life I have forced myself to forget.

That's the funny thing about trauma. You forget. I can literally, and have literally, forced myself to lock away memories because to revisit those places is to revisit a place of deep pain for me. I learned how to lock memories away in dark cages. I know that's not always the healthiest way to deal with things. I do. But you learn how to shut areas of yourself off, hide them away in the deep abyss of the mind, never to visit them again. Everybody does, really. But for us, we have in some sense learned how to do it for so long; our parents, and their parents, and their parents have passed down the lessons of survival: Lock it away, keep moving. It is what it is.

This one. I couldn't lock away. I couldn't forget.

.   .   .

HAVING TO FACE WHAT I HAD BECOME OVER THE PAST few years and the terrible ways I had learned to lie and to deflect and to run and to face myself again really opened up areas in my life that I thought I had already moved on from. Being around evangelicals became a way to cope with my feelings of being devalued and unseen. Going to church was a way of me running from the wounds I caused in my life.

Writing was a way for me to stop running and stop wounding and start healing.

Last year, I had been in a conversation with a friend about all that was going on in my life and what I felt I was seeing of myself in the mirror. He told me that anger reveals a lot of pain. It reveals that something just doesn't feel fair or right or equal in our lives, and so our job is to learn how to heal. He told me the story of Moses and all the ways Moses learned how to not face himself. He told me that God met Moses in his most vulnerable place and showed that he was still broken. He told me that I needed to make sense of my breaks. I had wondered what made me run so much. I had wondered what made me try to prove myself so much. I had wondered what made me break and bend. I had wondered what made me break and bend others. So I called my sister, because I knew that she might not be able to heal me and put me back together again, but at least she could listen, and I knew that that would be more than enough.

"You remember when I said 'Daddy, I can walk fast' at the baseball game?" I asked her.

"Yeah, boyyyy"—she always called me boy—"I remember that."

"Yeah, I just thought about that the other day." My mind went back to that cool evening, the lights in the distance, the darkness of outside the stadium as we made our way to the ticket gate. We were going to see the Capital City Bombers. My father loved to take us to baseball games whenever he got a chance. He would take us to junkyards. He would take us to old antiques stores. He would take us to pawn shops. He would take us wherever he could when he wasn't working long hours and late shifts at Walmart. For him, and for us, the Bombers had become our favorite baseball team. I didn't know any baseball. I didn't know how to read the score. I just knew they were my favorite.

"They really got on you. Didn't Depaul call you 'gay' or something? Didn't they get on you because you was 'switching' or something?" she said.

"Yeah, he did," I said with a laugh. "Yeah, I remember that. I'll never forget it. I don't think I realized how much that shaped me." I told her I thought about all the other young Black boys, both at school and at church, who don't easily fit into the "masculine" mold. Between locker rooms and lockers in school hallways, between the gas station and the altar, they were told very clearly that they were "other." We knew who they were. We knew what they were going through, but too often, what we knew didn't make us more loving or more understanding or more tender, for that matter.

"I know he was joking, but I know it ain't funny," she said, turning to grab something from the refrigerator.

"Yeah." A silent pause.

As we talked, my mind went back. I was terrified. I felt the same churning in my stomach and the same shivering in my fingers that I felt when I first laid eyes on Alton. It wasn't a badge or a bullet that made me shake. It was the possibility of revisiting a memory that I had locked deep inside of me. She was talking, but my eyes began to glaze. There was so much I wanted to say but didn't. My body, not quite a shivering, not quite still, just real uneasy, had so much more to say. My mind may have tried to forget, but my body couldn't. The longer we sat there, the more I started to feel the weight of anxiety come over me. The tears that I had buried deep within me started to well up.

I hated every bit of it. I hated what that did to me. I hated the way it made me feel, how much it made me always check myself, my hands, my hips, my legs, my face in the mirror as I tried to make sense of those words. I think it was the first time I actually felt like I hated myself, like there was something wrong with me because of what happened. Something as ordinary as language, syllables, letters making sentences, were powerful enough to make my little Black boy body a hated Black boy body.

"Aite, Domi," I said to her, as I grabbed my phone. "I got to get off." She looked at me and told me about the last pair of Jordans she got and the next pair of Jordans she was going to get. I told her that I would call her back. She told me that she loved me. I told her that I loved her, too. I hung up. That was a lie. I didn't have to go, but I did have to run.

The more I think about Alton and Philando, and the more I think about myself, and the more I think about all the Black boys who have been terrified, who have been hurt, it has made me really think hard about making sense of my own terror and my own hurt.

The ways we Black boys were treated as kids did not just somehow magically change when we went down in Jesus's name and came up wet, or when we put on a helmet and our names were across our backs, or when we opened up our Bibles and mouths from pulpits. We did not change, either. The same way we learned that we were hated was the same way we learned to distrust ourselves, as I did, and learned how to distrust one another. The same way we learned how to hide and to think that everything was okay and that we didn't have to tell anyone about the pain we were in. And we didn't have to tell anyone about how much we failed and we didn't have to tell anyone about how much we were trying not to be hated in the same way we learned how to become what people hated in us and what we hated in ourselves.

The way I treated my teammate when he didn't want to move, the way I was cold to Jas when she needed me most. The way I got comfortable with white hugs and white applause.

Black boys learn sexism, toxic masculinity, homophobia, and self-shame real early. We are caught between words that wound our spirits and systems that wound our bodies. We never really learn how to use our bodies, how to love our bodies, how to see that our bodies carry both glory and guilt, a complexity I'm still trying to wrap my mind around. We learn how to judge the worth and the value of other Black boys by how well we can approximate to standards of maleness that none of us can really fully achieve. We know this.

Yet, we try and we fail, and we come up with some how-to guide to make ourselves believe that we are becoming less sexist, less toxic, less homophobic, less shameful, more loving, more caring. We don't grow up being free like other children, able to find our way and have fun and make mistakes and grow up to be human like others. We must be rigid. Caught under the threat of the codes. You know, like we can't hug, or say "I love you," or if we do, we have to follow it up quickly with "no homo," straightening up, making jokes at one another, not knowing how all of it is killing us slowly. As boys whose bodies have been long abused in this country, stolen, raped, locked up, trying to get free from cages built for us, we learn how to perpetuate in ourselves the world that white supremacy and anti-Blackness built. We learn how we are just statistics, at least that's what we hear every time we gather in large crowds, don't feel like doing homework, walking home from school, going to college, getting shot dead selling CDs, shot dead with hoodies and candy, shot dead in white shirts and blue jeans.

We learn to walk in America not as whole and healthy humans, capable of loving and receiving love, but as wounded Black boys, Black boys who learn how to run and to hide as well as we learn how to run and to juke, or run and jump, run and sell, run and study, and run and hurt.

I believe we haven't been given space to heal from centuries of anti-Blackness. We just haven't been given the freedom to love our bodies deeply. In many ways, there is even a struggle to believe the image of God is upon this Black body. We have been so used to seeing dead Black bodies in the streets that we often miss living Black bodies in the shadows, hiding, just hoping someone would care enough to ask about their wounds and would love them enough to try to heal them. Bodies that have been called names, bodies that have been bullied, bodies that have been told about how much trouble they are bound for, bodies that have been singing and dancing, talking noise over *Madden* and *Mortal Kombat,* bodies that learn how to straighten up, bodies that just want to breathe. We have been so used to running fast, jumping high, getting the grades, escaping the most painful parts of ourselves and what has happened to us. It is not our fault. We must face ourselves and this damage for us to heal. We are not okay. That's okay. But we must confront the pain. As we confront the pain in our lives, as we face reality, bell hooks writes, we can take the broken bits and pieces and make ourselves whole again. Like Jesus, we can be healers.

I KNEW THAT DAY MY BROTHER DEPAUL WAS JUST JOK-
ing.

I know he really didn't mean it.

I know what this country and its people have done to him. How it made him laugh off the pain of those giving him lectures about how bad he was or how bad things could get. He had to figure out a way to shift some of the weight he was carrying on his shoulders—better yet, the weight he was carrying on his heart—as he tried to cry out for help, even when no one would hear him. Sadly some of those people didn't really want to love him; they saw him only as one of those thugs. You know, like the Bone Thugs-

N-Harmony song when the preacher came on the track and instead of preaching the liberating gospel, the only good news he had was what he was against. "We're not against rap," his voice came over the track, like an old Baptist sermon over vinyl. "We're not against rappers. . . . But we are . . . against . . . those . . . thugs."

Instead of passing on to people like my Black brother a legacy of protest, they taught them that the real enemy wasn't the system. The problems were them, with their oversized shirts, ghetto tattoos, and loud-ass music. So I get why my brother joked. Like they say, sometimes you have to laugh to keep from seeing the pain.

But that pain goes somewhere, and that means it usually goes to other people. Just so happened, on that unlucky day, I was that person. That hurt me. Not because my brother called me gay, but because I knew that it was something that he saw in me that he didn't like. I looked up to my brother a lot. Like, a lot. Everywhere I went, I was "Paul's brother." My brother was super athletic, fast, and he could fight, so being identified as his younger brother meant I was somebody. It meant that I would be protected. Other kids didn't really bother me because they knew who my brother was. They knew Paul. I did, too. And I loved my brother; he was that dude. He was that dude, foreal foreal. Until this day, I want to be the father that he is. He has shown so much courage, so much grace, so much faith, so much courage. He isn't perfect, and I ain't trying to save him from what he did that day. It just is what it is.

I HUNG MY WRIST AS A KID AND WAS ALWAYS TOLD NOT to be like "that." *That* meaning, not being like "those" boys, those gay boys. The people who told me this were in the church. They preached and served week in and week out. They prayed their prayers, anointed themselves with oil, anointed us with oil, and tried to love us deeply. I learned that God didn't like or love those gay Black boys they always warned us against. They were not image bearers first. They must stay wounded, wounded by those whom God tasked with loving them deeply into wholeness. That didn't often happen. Rarely. Young Black boys and young Black girls were "sat down," punished, abused. I learned that white people weren't the only ones who learned how to hurt Black bodies and wound Black spirits. I learned that lesson sadly, and I perpetuated the hurt. Sadly, so. I learned what bodies were meant to be loved and what bodies were meant to be punished. There were no eunuchs, as we find in the Bible, in our categories. No people who were fully human, fully different, and fully worthy of the deepest and most profound love.

From that event, I learned that loving myself as a kid required always proving who I was not. I learned to straighten up my walk and my talk. I learned to make sure I kept my hands at my side lest I get picked on for hanging my wrist. If I'm honest, so much pressure and so much proving and the ways I would be made to feel like an "other" the same way other Black boys did made me angry. I couldn't quite understand why my brother would call me gay and why my family members would always be trying to straighten me up, when I was just a kid trying to play video games, and football in my grandmother's yard, and racing my cousins in the road. It made me so angry that one day I joined in beating up another kid, a child like us, that we suspected of being gay. I joined in, lest I get bullied once again. Now I had my chance. We all got off the bus that day. It was a normal day after school. We all would be joking, talking about everything that happened that day, getting ready to play the wrestling game. We spotted the kid and chased him with sticks that we picked up from the side of the road.

And we ran after him.

I will never forget the terror that was in his face. His eyes widened. He was gasping, running.

It was like he was running for his life.

He was.

He was running from us.

He wanted, like many children, to get away from people trying to hurt him.

People who looked like him.

And we chased him. And we chased him.

He ducked and dodged and we chased him.

We finally got tired and stopped.

We yelled out, "Gay-ass nigga." We all looked at each other, me fake punching another in the chest, laughing. We all laughed. We knew that we were making good on the lessons that we caught between prayer meetings, long, hot sermons, conversations over tomatoes and rice, walking in the hallways, early morning rides on the bus, shouting about video games and how much we hated going to church: Jesus didn't love gay-ass niggas.

That day, I learned to perpetuate the violence against Black bodies. I learned that I was capable of violence, comfortable leaving wounded bodies to pick up the pieces of their own selves. And I didn't just wound; I learned how to bring God on the side of our violence. I learned too late, as James Baldwin, who struggled deeply with religious abuse to his Black queerness, wrote, that Jesus had nothing to do with it. Jesus, Baldwin writes, "would never have done that to me, nor attempted to make my salvation a matter for blackmail."

Jesus loves bodies, no matter who or where or what they are. And Jesus does not hurt people in order to love them. He did not live out of his own roundedness; he did not cover up his pain by enacting it onto others. Love did not need to hurt me. Love did not need to hurt my brother. Love did not need the other kid hurt. Jesus wanted us to learn love, and we never could quite figure it out. I learned too late, but I learned. I learned that we all live in brokenness, deep brokenness. I learned that Jesus does not forget bodies, despised and abused bodies, but becomes good news to them by remembering them, touching them and being touched, and creating a world where their bodies are liberated, redeemed, and resurrected.

COMING OF AGE IN A TIME OF PUBLIC LYNCHINGS HAS made me realize that I need more than words in those moments. I want to feel love. I want to feel loved in all the ways that I feel love has failed. I want to know that in this country bodies like ours will be loved.

Serious love. We need what Jesus called *neighbor love*. We need what Martin Luther King, Jr., called *redemptive love*. We need what Toni Morrison called *self love*. We need what bell hooks called *committed love*. We need what Kiese Laymon calls *responsible love*.

James Baldwin was right: Love did not begin and end the way we thought it did. Love is war. Love is about growing up. It is about facing ourselves and our country and exposing the ways both fail to love us.

I knew that though this country and even the church did not love us, the least I could do was try to.

In 2017, I started teaching middle school at a local

Christian school. Jas and I were so excited because it was not only going to give me a way to provide for the family, but she also knew how much I loved being around the next generation and walking alongside them as I did as a coach when we were in California. When I became a coach, I was determined to make sure that the kids felt like they mattered and that they felt loved in all the ways I felt loved by my coaches growing up. It started off as a good experience. Though I wasn't necessarily comfortable around white people anymore, there were a lot of Black kids there that made me really want to teach there.

When I first showed up to the school, having been invited by a member of the church, the director of the school kept telling me about all the ways they wanted to see Black kids succeed and grow up and be responsible husbands and responsible wives and responsible Christians. I never really questioned her authenticity because, as many white people do, she pointed out to me all of her ten books by Black people she had read, one of them being my favorite, Howard Thurman's *Jesus and the Disinherited*. I can remember her walking me around the school, the hardwood floors creaking with each step, and me hearing the voices of laughter as I passed one door, a teacher pointing to the board at another, a young kid walking by me dapping me up as we made our way upstairs. As the only Black middle-school teacher at an otherwise white school, I knew that I could learn to love these young children; they would need to feel heard and protected, challenged and honored.

My mom would always show us documentaries as kids or take us to the Black museums whenever we would go to Memphis or Atlanta or up to Baltimore to visit family and visit churches that were in our fellowship. "We're going to the King museum," she would say. "Today," she said, as she turned on the television, sitting us down with our lunch that she had made earlier, "today, we're going to look at *Eyes on the Prize*." We were excited. It was a serious moment, as serious as she told us to enter our Pentecostal church, as serious as she told us to make sure we acted right at school. There was a copy of Alice Walker's *The Color Purple* on the table beside the couch we sat on. It was old and beat up, the creases showing that the book had been read over and over again. There were other books as well, but *The Color Purple* stood out the most. I asked her some time ago if I could take it with me, since I was going to be writing on Alice Walker's work, Black literature, and Black theology.

"Nope," she responded, smiling and then laughing. "No, I can't let you take that one." I was okay. I agreed that, more than I needed it for writing, she needed it to remind her of all the ways Black women were treated, and all the ways Alice Walker reminded them that they were loved, and all the ways she told them that their wounds could become worlds and that the world would be a better place if the world listened to Black women as much as they listened to God.

She was a nurse in a middle school. I remember riding with her to her school while I was in high school and even when I came home from college, and her introducing me as her baby boy to all of her co-workers. She was the healer of the school. Kids came in, aggravating her about things that really didn't hurt, just so that they, as we did as kids, could get out of solving the next equation that didn't really solve things in life. I remember being there one time and her talking softly to one of the children, as if the child was her own, pulling out a story from her memory, telling the child the story, and sending the child back to her classroom. The child came in with her face bent like she smelled some bad milk. The child left with her face smooth and grinning like she just ate a lollipop or saw the tooth fairy. My mother had a way with turning bad things into something beautiful. I guess Alice Walker taught her that as well. I guess she taught my momma that Black women took words meant to break them like "womanish" and turned them into worlds that loved them. Her room, the small, old-smelling nurse's office, was full of love, like Alice said: "Loves music. Loves dance. Loves the moon. Loves the Spirit. Loves love and food and roundness. Loves struggle. Loves the Folk. Loves herself. Regardless."

So when I took the job, when I came to school in my outfits from H&M, I wanted to be like my momma. I wanted to introduce my kids to Black folk. I wanted to teach them to love music, love dance, love the world, love themselves, love the people, regardless of ways that they had learned not to love music, not learned how to dance, not felt love in the world, not loved themselves, and not loved the people around them.

Even if they didn't know, I knew I was entering a space where there would be Black boys and Black girls, white boys and white girls, just like my brother, me, and the young kid we wounded. Each of us would be caught up somehow in this web of violence all around us, trying to find healing and hope. We all were caught up in this unloving world, trying to make classrooms turn into altars where we could offer ourselves a better story than the one that was offered to us. Each of us would need to find a way to imagine better for ourselves and others. All of us would be looking for somebody to really be Jesus to us. To love us, to listen, to understand, to protect, to inspire, and to shape us. To hold us when we are struggling and to stand with us when we are alone. That's what I knew I had to do. I knew I had to teach them to be different.

I was trying to protect them, knowing what this world could do to them, knowing what people who looked like them would do, knowing even the ways the adults that they looked up to would also hurt them, and somehow they, too, would have to learn how to find ways to love themselves. I knew that there were so many different webs that they could get caught up in, where they would be wound up, and the spinning, instead of putting their beauty on display, would mean their destruction. I knew that I couldn't be their parents. That is a sacred place.

I could never get why so many said that teachers are parents. Some of us were, yes, to our own children. But to another, we don't get to have that, no matter how bad we think their parents are doing. We don't get to be the ones who snatch babies from the bosom of their mothers and fathers thinking that we know what's best. We as teachers are trained in perfection, getting the answer right, judging another's progress on whether or not they can recall some number or some day. And these children didn't need perfection. They carried enough weight, pressing on their small shoulders, bent out of shape, still moving. They didn't need that.

They needed love.

REGGIE (LET'S JUST CALL HIM THAT) HAD ENTERED MY office one morning, just as the day was getting started. He was short, slim, his face brown like caramel. His hair was cut in a fade. He wore the blue top and khaki bottoms that was the school uniform. He would always talk to me about the latest Steph Curry highlight that was on Instagram, the latest update in *Fortnite,* or the girls that he had been thinking about slipping notes to, or ask to play basketball during lunchtime. I would laugh at him because I was reminded of my childish love with Jas in college, when I would plan to cross paths with her, or plan to ask her out to the movies, or plan to catch eyes with her as she sang and I played the drums during gospel choir rehearsal. There was something so pure about his desire for love. There was something so young but so honest about the way he thought he was the best-looking dude in the school, better looking than all the other dudes, with the same fade in their heads, and the same blue shirt with HERITAGE ACADEMY on the left side of it, and the same khaki bottoms.

On this otherwise uneventful morning, I could tell that something was bothering him. His face was not adorned with his bright smile, his white teeth glistening, and the way his body would sway side to side, up and down, almost like he was trying to show that he commanded the space. I could tell he was in pain. His mouth didn't say much, but his body said so much more.

"Mr. Stew," he called out to me the way he would when it was time to talk about some real stuff. "Can I holla at you for a second?"

"Of course," I said as I made some space at my desk. I would get to school early and try to either work on some essays that I had been thinking about or finish lesson plans that I was working on. This particular morning I was working on a lesson to teach them about Martin Luther King, Jr., since MLK Day was coming up. I had taken a look at the previous year's Bible curriculum and realized that none of the kids were learning about Black people the way we'd learned, none of them were learning about justice the way we'd learned, and none of them were learning about ways Christians were to be loving neighbors and do whatever we could to make the country more loving and more just. So I decided to do what I could to help introduce them to the journey I was taking. I knew I couldn't teach them just about how to be better Christians; I had to help them learn how to be better humans and better Americans. Sometimes that meant playing a video of a protest and getting their thoughts. Sometimes that meant listening to a sermon and having them talk about it. Sometimes that meant reading and learning about the Bible. Sometimes that meant learning history. And sometimes it meant just being there for them, just to listen and talk about whatever they wanted.

Reggie and I had gotten used to starting random conversations about life, about mommas and daddies, about loss, about sports, about poetry. He began to tell me about something he had done that he knew was going to get him in trouble. I assured him that he was just fine with me. I made sure that he knew I couldn't save him from whatever he did, but that I could be there to talk with him.

"Now—" Reggie gave me that look, like he knew he was in trouble, but he knew he wanted to say something about it. "Mr. Stew, I ain't meant it like that," he pleaded. "I didn't even do anything," he said.

I looked at him. I looked down at my journal. "You didn't?" I asked.

"Mr. Stew," he said, "you don't believe me?"

When he asked me that, my mind went back to when I'd asked the same question of a teacher at school. "Well, I don't know yet," I told him, as I shuffled some papers around. "It's not about whether I believe you or not. It's about whether or not you telling the truth to yourself."

He looked at me, partly confused, partly about to grab his stuff. "Mr. Stew," he said, "you always trying to teach us lessons."

I agreed. I told him that was my job, that's what they paid me for, and that's what put food on my table. "You don't want to learn?" I asked.

"Of course," he told me, his mouth twisting a bit into a smile.

"Aite then," I told him. "Learning means listening to lessons. I don't know the situation, nor do I want to know it, but I will tell you what I think." We walked toward the door. "I'm not saying I'm right.

I'm just saying I been where you been and done learned some things the hard way and learned some things the not-so-hard way."

He walked out of my room and went downstairs. "Mr. Stew," he said to me, looking my way, pulling his backpack more on his back, "you alright with me."

I walked out of the room and thought about all the conversations I'd had with teachers where they didn't have answers, but they'd at least tried to make things all right even if they weren't.

I don't know if it was because I was one of the youngest teachers or the only Black male teacher in the entire school or that I played sports, but there was something about me that Reggie gravitated to. I tried not to assume too much about my students. In so many of the conversations, many of the teachers lamented the *poor* kids, their *poor* families, and their *poor* morals. I knew none of that was true. Complex? Yes. Poor? Not at all.

There was richness, vibrancy, beauty, untapped potential, unlocked hope, shattered souls wanting to be whole again. From that day on, Reggie and I began to share conversations over meals. We shared conversations in the hallways, after class, on the basketball court, and more. The more he talked to me, the more we found ourselves overlapping things we loved, things we disliked, things we didn't necessarily understand, things that were just flat-out normal but meaningful.

He had a lot of questions about God, himself, his parents, his Blackness, his fears, his hopes, his poetry, his friends, how much he hated school uniforms, teachers who singled him out, and missing out on the *good* lunch. He had gotten tired of lying, tired of running, tired of ducking and dodging, tired of hiding his pain. He was a young man that was part hurt and part angry. I learned that he felt others blamed him too much. He was so afraid of failure, so afraid—lest he become, as teachers would often say, like "those guys" (insert *troublemaker, thug,* or whatever characterization white people give Black boys to feel better about calling them a *nigger*). He told stories of painful events that had happened in his life and how those painful events informed how he saw the world.

The other teachers didn't see that, though. Instead they warned me about him, called him a troublemaker based on his past report cards.

But he wasn't. He was a kid who wanted to feel seen. He wanted things to be all right. He was a Black boy, just like me, trying to learn, trying to get girls, trying to show how he was the best-looking thing walking, trying to run rather than facing problems.

He was *just like me*.

"Mr. Stew," he asked me one day on the basketball court. "What you think about Juice WRLD?"

"I don't know," I said. "Who is that?"

"Come on, mannn, Mr. Stew, you don't know Juice?" he said. He sucked his teeth and laughed at the thought of me not knowing Juice.

"His music be hitting, no cap," he told me.

"Aite, I'll listen to him," I said, as I pulled out my phone and opened up YouTube. "What should I listen to?" I asked.

"Let's see." He paused for a little, his mind going through Juice's portfolio. "Start with 'Lucid Dreams,'" he told me.

"Aite, I will," I said. "What makes 'Lucid Dreams' so good?" I asked.

He looked at me. He looked down. He looked at me again. "Well, for me, his music is real. He is real about his pain and how he cope. Now, I ain't saying it's right the way he does it," he told me. "But at least he's real and he's actually honest.

"You remember how you told us about Jesus and him crying out in the garden?" he asked, reminding me of a gospel story I'd used in a lesson on honesty, pain, and hope. "You remember how you said we got to be honest to get better?"

"Yeah, I do."

"Well, that's what Juice and Jesus did . . . they were honest."

"Yeah, you right," I said.

"You always be making us think, Mr. Stew," he told me.

"We got to learn how to live here," I said as I thought about the space between his Black body, my Black body, the orange basketball, the concrete court. "That's what Juice was doing."

"Yeah, he was. He was a Black dude trying to learn how to live."

"That's faith," I told him. "Us Black dudes trying to learn how to be honest, find meaning in the story of Jesus, and live in this country."

"I feel that, Mr. Stew. No cap."

For some reason, the teachers were so hard on him. They would find any little thing to call his momma about or call him out for. Some of the teachers complained about him in the teachers' meeting. This never sat well with me. The image of white teachers talking about all the trouble a Black kid was giving them just didn't make my insides feel good. It was like he was in boot camp, rather than in an environment that loved wounded Black girl and boy bodies. I wonder, did he feel it? Did he hate it like I did? Did he struggle to love himself? Did they even know his story? Did they even know him? Did they love him?

By the time I was ready to have that conversation with the school staff, he was up for expulsion. It was toward the end of the school year. The administration had a meeting with him and his family. There was really nothing I could do, either to get them to care about him more or to save him from what he'd done.

As the weeks progressed, between the classroom and the basketball court, we had tried to figure out ways to speak about the life of faith together, him talking about the ways he hated going to church, dressing up in oversized suits like me, all the whooping and hollering the preacher did. I promised him that I would get on *Fortnite* and try it out. He was trying and trying and trying.

One night, as I was sitting in my study eating some curry that Jas had cooked, listening to John Coltrane and getting ready for the next day's lesson, my phone rang. "Mr. Stew." It was Reggie's mother. "Thank you," she said.

"Thank you for what?" I asked.

"You know he's been talking about you all the time. He's been going on and on about the things y'all been talking about."

"Yeah, he's pretty talented," I said as I told her what she already knew. "Did he show you his poem that he wrote the other day?"

"Nah, he didn't."

"Ask him to show it to you sometime when he's ready," I said. "He wrote a good one. I think he can really go somewhere. I really believe in him."

"I know you do. He tells me that all the time. Thank you, Mr. Stew. I mean it. Thank you."

"You're welcome. I know it's hard on him and you."

"Yeah, it is, but thank you," she repeated. "Thank you for being someone who really finally loved him."

"You're welcome."

We hung up.

I put the phone down.

I don't know if I actually did a good job at that. But at least I know I tried. I tried to see myself in him and all the children who were just trying to survive, trying to live in between threats and lessons, hallelujahs and patriotic anthems, school uniforms and basketball shorts, dead Black bodies and Black bodies screaming in the streets, white boys with badges, white boys with Bibles, white boys with bullets, and a country that didn't quite understand the meaning of love. I knew I couldn't protect him. I couldn't protect myself. I couldn't protect my brother. I couldn't protect my uncle. None of us could protect ourselves in places that were not concerned with our protection, but we could be loved.

We are all trying. We see the world burning. We've seen knees on necks, they've seen white guys in blue suits, gold badges, red flags, yelling, screaming. They've seen cold bodies, overtaken by fear, grief, death. They need us. We need them. Hold them. We are trying. Hungry stomachs churning, minds finding ways to cope through Chromebooks and black controllers, wondering if anybody is screaming from the inside like them. We both are scared. Our palms are sweating. Our hearts, racing. We are more than scared. We're angry. We're lonely.

I think about our kids so much. Even us, who still have faint memories of childhood we never dealt with. Places that have been haunting us, showing up like ghosts, coming and going. Going and coming. We are all wondering: Is there any place that is safe?

So we are all trying.

We are trying to hold one another, while our knees are weak, chests are tight, our worlds on fire, burning and burning and burning and burning. While we are all trying to simply exhale. Breathe. Even for a moment, in this place, that is enough. It is hard to fight; it's harder to breathe. When we find that breath—shallow, short, still going—we know there is still life there. And if there is life, there is joy, there is peace, there is struggle, there is faith, there is hope, there is something, something that keeps us living.

We believe, no matter how cold it is, that beautiful Black people must find beautiful Black love.

FLOODING.

The act of imagination is bound up with memory.
—TONI MORRISON

Five miles from the home I grew up in is my grandparents' old red brick house in Sandy Run, South Carolina. There are trees, paved roads giving way to beige dirt, old crushed soda cans; there are old rusty cars sitting on cinder blocks, and there are broken mailboxes held together by three or four nails. Ten miles from this house is the white-stained brick church in Swansea, South Carolina. The red carpet on the ground greets you as you enter, always in a suit, the best you can muster, the best you have. I don't know if there are maps that show these places, these old landmarks, as many of the old folk back home would say. I don't know if they show you the red brick house, and the old cars, and the brick porch with lights around it. I don't know if they show you the white-stained brick with mold traveling upward from the outside air-conditioning unit, or the people who travel between both.

But they are there.

Between these two places, the old red brick house that my granddaddy built, and the white-stained church that we called home, was where my grandmother and I would talk about things we remembered. Things that were familiar to both of us. Things that only she knew. Things that I'd only heard of. Things I wanted to say to her but didn't know how. Really, the distance between us was not very far, but felt colossal, foreign even. There was a part of her that I could see in her dark brown eyes and rough hands smoothed by Vaseline that I didn't know.

She rarely likes to talk about it, but she remembers.

When I became a teacher, I loved telling her about all the things I was learning about myself and about my kids and about lesson plans and how much I hated being at a place that struggled to care about teaching us and loving us. I would call her from time to time, just to talk about old memories and to ask her how she was doing, and how Granddaddy was doing, and how the weather was, and whether she'd started putting salt in her chicken again. When I have time I love to just go back home, enjoy her not-so-sweet tea, and her not-so-salty fried chicken. She says that she can't eat and drink like she used to because of the *sugar.*

One day I walk up to the porch, my foot missing the grass coming through the cracks, and I knock on the door.

"Hey, boy." My uncle Ralph, her brother, answers the door. His old body, much like my grandmother's, is frail, sort of bent out of shape. "Hey, Uncle Ralph," I say as he calls my cousin to grab the key. I walk in the old brick house, and I can smell nothing. I pass the white couch. There are pictures of everyone everywhere. I see pictures of me, my sister, my brothers, my cousins, near and distant. It is hot, it feels like I'm in the oven, yet nothing is on the stove. There is no food being cooked. There is the scent of nothingness, but it is familiar. I sit at the small table in the kitchen, looking around to see if there is anything to grab to eat, or even to drink. I haven't been here in so long, so I don't know where things are anymore.

I have always wanted to talk to her about the old days, trying to get a story of the reason why Uncle Sambo left, the reason why she stayed instead of migrating north like many of the Black folk did during those turbulent years of the 1940s, '50s, '60s, and '70s. I wanted to know what made Granddaddy take all those people and their children to vote when they first heard they were given the "right" to shape the country that did so much to her and others that looked like her. I wanted to tell her how angry I was about everything that was going on. I wanted to know how she and other Black folks made it through when they heard the news that Emmett Till's small Black body had been lynched and the "white man," as she called them, got off. I was searching for answers, like I would ask her as a kid. I was being that kid again. That small boy sitting at the table asking my grandma questions she probably ain't even know the answer to but still tried to answer because she knew how important that was.

She rarely likes to talk about it, but she remembers.

She remembers, but my granddaddy doesn't. Memory is something that he has lost. His memory is a faint picture, a brief yet piercing remembrance of younger days, traveling to El Paso, Texas, and to California for his military service. He repeats his stories over and over, trying to hold on to what pieces of his former self he has left. "I'm Danté, your grandson," I say. "Oh, okay, good to meet you," he says, as he laughs and rubs his old bald head with its patches of white on the side. He has dementia. It is hard as hell to watch. It is horror. All of the good times we had, his dancing like James Brown, stomping his feet while he played the piano, car rides and ball games, have faded away with each passing day. I know him, but he doesn't remember me.

My grandma is sharp. She is small, her body often covered in her long, old black trench coat. Her hair, streaks of gray and streaks of black, is usually covered by a scarf, and then by a hat because she never wants to be anywhere where she can pray and not have her head covered. Her eyes are deep brown, wrinkles could make you miss them. Her eyes are covered as well, with glasses, so that as she prays, she can see with her mind and with her eyes the things she can touch. She remembers so much. Every time I am around her, I just sit and listen, and listen at her tell old stories that feel as close as her hands when she prays. Her walk is slower now. She's not as fast as she used to be, but her mind is sharp, so sharp. She can access just about any memory in the blink of the eye, or at the flip of a coin, or as quick as she told me to fix my own food one time when Jas tried to fix it for me. I always laugh thinking about that. I don't know if she would call herself a Black feminist, or would even call herself wanting to liberate Jas from all the ways Black women have learned to serve Black men and white women and white men. All I know is that though she wanted Jas to love me and to help me, she didn't want her feeling like she had to fix my food.

She walks into the kitchen.

"Hey, Grandma," I say.

"Hey, boy," she says as she sorts through the local paper to get coupons for the Krogers, as she calls it. "How Jas and the baby?" she asks as she looks up with a smile on her face. She loves talking about my wife and my son. She loves her grandkids and great-grandkids, always smiling when she talks about us, calling us blessings.

"They are doing good. We aite." We talk a little more, about work at the school, and how I just took a job working at the local coffee shop, Buona Caffe. She never really did like hearing about coffee, but she loved hearing about all the people I was meeting, and all the books I told her I was reading in between making drinks, and all the stuff I was learning about myself and the kids. Every time I talked about something, she would relate it, once again, to a story or a lesson or something that took us back in time and in her life.

That's the thing about my grandma. I can be talking about something that happened in 2020 one minute, and be in 1951 the next. She lets you into the universe she's in, the things she's seen: the fat, sloppy, stank pigs and slaughterhouses she remembers as a kid, about Grandma Idealla, her mother, and about Uncle Walter, her brother, and about Jesus, and rides to town, and about how she covers her head to pray, and about voting, and about laws, and the things she been praying, and about the ways the country has not learned how to change. I just sit and listen. Somehow we just end up talking about everything; she is in her own world, and I'm enjoying every bit of it. Her memories flood, and we both are engulfed.

"Can you tell me a little bit about back then?" I ask.

She pauses, moving around some of the coupons from the newspaper she has on the table. "What do you mean?"

"Well," I say, trying to figure out actually what I mean, "my class and I was looking at a documentary about the civil rights movement."

"Um," she responds, not really giving an answer, or not really saying too many words. I have told her about all the documentaries I have watched over the years, and how inspired I have been, and how seeing Black people resist gave me strength for my own struggle, how I wanted to know how she, my grand-daddy, and all the other Black folk in the country had survived. She was not a person to really talk about all the stuff that happened to her and Black people back then.

"Didn't you say Granddaddy was, like, real active during that time or something?" I ask.

She smiles, this time fixing her glasses, taking them off, wiping the fog out with her shirt, and put-ting them back on again. "Yes, he was," she says. "He used to take all the people around town to vote. He used to pick them up," she tells me, her face smooth-ing out a bit. "He used to pick them up, and get them registered, and made sure they knew about who they were voting for and who was on the ballot." I begin to smile at the thought of my granddaddy actually being an activist. I had become inspired by so many Black folk and just the thought that one of those people was my granddaddy made me feel a lot better about me risking a lot for the ways I was trying to love us.

I walk into the living room. There's an old picture of me in my football uniform from high school. I have a little smirk on my face. I am holding a football in my right hand, my gloves are matching my socks, my jersey is oversized, and my knees have the cut-off socks on them to match my shirt underneath my jersey. To the right there was an award: NAACP SERVICE HOURS AWARD. The name beneath it: Johnny Albert, my granddaddy.

"Grandma," I say as I walk back into the kitchen. "You ever think y'all would be dealing with the same stuff we dealing with today? You ever thought things wouldn't get better?"

She pauses again. Her deep brown eyes looking at me with a seriousness as deep as those eyes. "We thought things would get better," she says, "but that's the world for you." She looks down and back up again. "That's the world."

She is Pentecostal, so everything that is evil and all the ways that Americans learned to hate and harm Black people is the work of the devil. This country is not God's country but the house of Satan. The wages of sin and suffering are on the face and on the body and in the eyes of every Black person that has survived American hatred. She said "the world," but what she was really saying is that this country learned to hate as well as they learned to say the name Jesus. The wages of sin was as glaring and as powerful and as real as was her body sitting down at the table with me.

I have not given much thought before this moment that my grandmother, who was born in the 1930s, saw signs that told Black people where they could and could not go, she saw the pictures of Emmett Till's distorted face, she saw and heard and participated in our people's struggle for freedom, she remembered what it was like not to be able to vote and then the next day sign your name and cast your ballot, she remembered the murders, the backlash, the retrenchment, the insatiable desire of the country for our destruction. She remembered our resistance and the ways we used our bodies and our ballots to write a different story, a story of this country that would say Black people were worthy of living, and loving, and worth fighting for. She lived to see a Black man, and a Black woman, and their Black daughters, walk and live in the White House. She lived through it all, and so much of the world that she hated remembering and which hated her, was still around, and she did not want to talk about it but she did, and I would be able to listen and to find something of meaning in my own hatred of retelling stories and reliving them.

"Thank you, Grandma," I say, as I walk outside to my truck to grab my books. "Thank you."

She looks at me, with those same deep brown

eyes, and says, "Danté, you know I always like talking to you." I always like to talk. She always likes to talk. We both love to talk and avoid and not relive and learn and listen together.

I come back into the house and open up my journal and write some words. I open up my book, June Jordan's *Technical Difficulties.* I read a few pages. I open up my journal and take a few notes. I just can't get out of my mind, as she talks: *How in the world did they have to witness the brutal murder of Emmett Till and Malcolm X and Martin and Eric Garner and Sandra Bland and Trayvon and Alton and Philando? What did it do to them? Why has this country not done anything to stop it? Is she as angry as I am? What is she feeling? What did she remember? Can she tell? Does she want to tell me?* What I really wanted to say is, "Grandma, I don't know if I know how to survive."

Margaret Elizabeth Albert, my grandmother, a Black woman from rural South Carolina, survived this country. She survived. Johnny Rubin Albert, my granddaddy, a Black man from rural South Carolina, survived. Debra Stewart, my momma, a Black woman from rural South Carolina, and her eight sisters and brothers survived. Calvin Stewart, my daddy, a Black man from rural South Carolina, and all his brothers and sisters survived. All the Black folk between that red brick house and that white-stained brick church survived.

I wondered what made them survive. They had

been through so much scaring and wounding. Their minds had burned on them images of terror, and images of triumph, and images of struggle, and images of love, and images that could not escape them even if they tried. I wondered what made them love themselves so deeply. I wondered what kept them together as their bodies and their hearts were shattered to pieces. I wondered if I could overcome the shattering, if I could pick up the pieces, and begin again, and hope again. I just kept wondering. Was it the prayers that I heard them wailing during those noondays? Was it a mix of fried chicken, fried livers, and fried fish, and green beans and pork 'n' beans and rice? Was it the sweaty sermons and shouting with long stockings? Was it leaving school early, marching, and protesting? Was it the anointing oil, the Blood, the Holy Ghost? Was it rage? Was it love? Was it just ordinary? Was it nothing? I don't know, but I know all of us were still here, breathing, sometimes labored, sometimes relaxed, sometimes still. Some of us were passing memories and faded silhouettes of a time long gone.

Since I'd left the white church, I was hungry to go back to the body where I came from: the Emmanuel Church of Our Lord Jesus Christ; our songs of praise; Bishop's fevered altar calls; tongues ablaze. All the smells of cheap cologne and fried chicken waiting after service. All the memories we had and terrible ways we learned and all the ways we learned how to forget and all the ways we learned how to be better. Every word, every smell, every moment a love letter, an epistle of hope, a gospel story in these strange lands. I had missed it all. And I had learned to hate it all. I had learned to run and to hide and to be embarrassed by such audacious claims to Blackness. I had learned to not love the smells and hate the songs and hate altar calls and bridle my tongue. All the memories of bodies being healed and all the memories of bodies dancing and all the memories of bodies being ordinary and human and tender and terrible just like others, all these memories I wanted to forget, never to relive. I thought my power would be found in silencing this, in keeping these memories contained to the past. But the truth is, I've never seen anything as beautiful as this. I had missed it all. I wanted it back and I didn't have it. I wanted it back in all the ways that I had lost it. I wanted it back in all the ways I learned how to destroy it. I wanted it back because I didn't want to let white people have any part of me anymore. I wanted it back because I wanted to regain what I felt I had lost, with every word by a white theologian, and every song coming from white lips, and every criticism about Black people that came from us, and all the shame, and all the terror, and all the being human, I wanted it back. I had been sad about all that my parents and grandparents had suffered. I had crucified the beautiful things they offered in order to be loved by white people and to feel that

I matter and had a place here. I was terrified. I was terrified because I saw what the country had done to them and did to me. I was terrified because the way they faced themselves is the way I would have to face myself. I was terrified because I know this cruel, loveless world took so much from them. I was terrified because they loved and I don't know if I loved in a way that honored them and loved them in ways that healed them and made them feel like they mattered as much as they made me feel like I mattered. I was afraid somewhere deep down inside that I would never get it back. I felt that it was only a memory that I would reach for to prove myself and to find some way to love myself when I couldn't find a way and when I couldn't remember.

Nostalgia is a powerful tool of ignorance and retrenchment of the social order. In America, white folk have been hooked on memories that somehow made the country look better than it was, that allowed white people to remain innocent in a country that has always been confused about Black folk and committed to white folk. Those who looked like us, as Viet Thanh Nguyen writes of Vietnamese civilians during the war, were seen but seen *through*. Visible yet invisible. American yet not American. Free yet not free. Here yet not seen. Needed yet exploited. Saved yet condemned.

But nostalgia, *white* nostalgia, erases people like my grandmother, who was sitting in front of me, holding on to what memories she had, what memories she wanted to forget, what memories she wanted to tell. It erases people like Trayvon, people like Alton, people like Philando. The project of white supremacy has always been a project of erasure, sweeping under the rugs, wiping away from pages, actively distorting the story of us, what Nguyen calls *unjust forgetting*. White folk wanted to forget. They wanted to baptize themselves in American lies, and American gospels, and American sermons, and American anthems. It was not an accident. It was an act of terror.

My grandma held on to her memories, but she did not hold on to the myths the country tried to get her and other Black people to believe. She didn't hold on to myths that made her more violent, less loving, more hate filled and less compassionate. She went back in time but she did not want to stay there. She went back to hold on to the beautiful parts of her story and the beautiful parts of the country, but she was not into protecting any type of innocence, either for herself, her country, or white people in this country. Her body was a memorial. Her memories a testament. Both read: I survived the worst of this country. But she said so much more. Her body and her memories were a testament of love, deep love for Black people. This was not erasure of the Black body and Black memories, as so many white people have done, but this was holding on to what has been lost, letting go of what can't be changed, and creating something better even in the midst of brutality. She was not nostalgic that way like so many Americans. How could she be? She was not trusting of this country as other people were, believing that it wanted what's best for people like us. The Lord might not have failed her, as she would tell me over and over again in between stories, but this country did. She was skeptical because she remembered. Remembering was war. And in war, Nguyen says, battles are fought twice: the first time on the battlefield, the second time in memory.

It was a battle both for the country and a battle for the survival of her body and her mind and her children and their children. It was a battle to force the church and country to see the ways in which our bodies were abused and forgotten. It was a battle to force the people of this country to see our humanity and their inhumanity, which they were creative at denying and evading. And because she remembered, I feel like she didn't want to tell me the story of survival; she wanted to show me. With presence. Her presence was the story of survival. It was the equipment of protection, a sort of sword and shield.

Every time I would go home, I would try to get whatever I could out of her.

"Grandma, tell me more about back then," I started asking anytime I saw her.

"What do you want to know?" she'd ask. And

then an entire universe—an entire devastating and hopeful universe—would soon form from the stories she'd share.

As a writer, the more I read Baldwin and Morrison, the more I realized how important it was to preserve our stories. I was reading book after book in seminary, but none of them took seriously my grandma and her story. Even if they didn't, I knew that I could. So I tried to talk to her and have her open up as much as she liked. "If you don't feel like talking about it," I told her, faking like I didn't really want to know, "you don't have to." But I wanted her to; I wanted her to so bad.

She paused.

She gave out a little laugh.

She rubbed her rough, greasy hands together.

She paused again. She laughed again.

We went back to talking about something else.

She rarely likes to talk about it, but she remembers.

I could tell she kind of wanted to talk to me and kind of didn't want to talk to me. "I'm going through a little bit right now," she said. "You're going to have to give me some time." I was all right with that. I could spare some time to get a story out of her. My family is full of storytellers. My momma is a storyteller. My daddy is a storyteller. My aunts are storytellers. My uncles are storytellers. They all would somehow sneak a story of some old uncle getting chased out the house with a gun, or something that happened in church, or something about what the *white man* did. Between that red brick house and that white-stained brick church were a lot of stories. Sometimes they were lessons I wasn't feeling. Sometimes they were dumb and irrelevant. What mattered was they were ours. Stories really are the material that hold us together; it is the oxygen that keeps our bodies going.

My grandma hated going back in time, though, so she hated when I asked about the stories back then. She hated revisiting stories of trauma. I wanted to talk. She just wanted to rest and to lock it away in her mind, never to face it again, or never to let it face her. She had a right. "We have been dreaming of freedom," professor and activist Brittney Cooper writes, "and carving out spaces for liberation since we arrived on these shores."

My grandma has been carving out space with those rough, greasy hands wherever she could. She may not have said it with her mouth, but her body was saying so much more. Her body hated the smells. Her body hated the feeling. There would be an uneasiness that came upon her spirit; I could see her frail body tense up. The woman that I had known to rub her thighs and her knees when the Holy Ghost got a hold of her in church, the high-pitched laugh that she gave over our conversations about things she found funny, laughing as she was making unsalted chicken, each of those had left her as quick as the memory came to her.

She fixed her long blue skirt, rolled up her sleeves, fixed her glasses, and she looked at me and gave me a smile, really a smirk, as we sat at the kitchen table.

When she began telling me about that day—the March on Washington, the "I Have a Dream" speech—her body was not bent anymore; it was upright, erected as a pledge of love. I could see joy come over her body as she took this trip. She was so proud then; she was so proud now. "We all gathered around the television," she said. "We were watching everybody give their speeches." She talked about how he was in front of all those people bearing witness. She said the Spirit of the Lord came upon him that day. She said it was different. She said Black folk felt free.

"We were so proud of Martin," she said. "He was preaching. Black folk felt good." She emphasized the good. She always emphasized the good and feeling good and being good. "I remember when the Civil Rights Act was passed." I'm just looking at her. "Your granddaddy, when the Voting Rights Act was passed," she said, "went all around this neighborhood to make sure all the Black folk were registered to vote. He made sure he took his truck around the neighborhood to get everybody to go vote."

I didn't really want to talk to her about Martin. I knew how she felt about that day. "Boy . . . it was like the earth stood still," my daddy said when I'd asked him about that day. So I left that one alone.

"Grandma, you got to tell me about white folk." I wasn't really looking for history events, but the emotions, the war, the wounds. "What was it like to live around white people back then?" I asked.

But her body bent over again, curling under the weights. She didn't want to talk about it again. "Okay, that's fine," I said. "Maybe another time." I kept trying to get something to take back with me. She kept trying to get somewhere safe. Both of us were trying to move beyond what white people did to us. Life was so much more than the terrible things they had imagined or actually accomplished or we tried to forget. Both of us know what was true of us, but the wounds were already there. Showing up again and again.

"Grandma," I said, as she fixed some tea and I sat at the table, "a lot of people are talking about how this country is great."

"Great for who?"

"Great for us."

"I don't know about that," she responded.

"Me either." Like most Black folk her age, she keeps a picture of President Obama, Michelle, Malia, and Sasha in the living room. It is big. It is beautiful. It sits next to a picture of who, as a kid, I always thought to be Dr. J, the basketball player. It sits near my grandfather's awards. I wonder if it is a reminder of Black people's deep love for ourselves, our arts, our sports, and our country. Barack is in his black suit, white shirt, blue tie; Michelle in her dress the color of a flower, a deep and abiding red like roses, with shiny pearls around her neck. The children, like children, just like us. For some he represented a sellout, somebody who didn't stand up for Black people when they needed it most. For others he represented them losing the country they thought was theirs, a sort of symbol of the destruction of white supremacy. Still for others, he represented our shining prince, the resurrection of Black racial politics, part Martin, part Malcolm, part sermon, part jeremiad. Still for others, he represented just another nigga who made it, nothing more, nothing less.

I pointed to the picture and asked her how it made her feel. "God is good, Danté," she said. "God is good." I agreed. We both knew that though this is America and America stayed on fire, God was still in the midst of it all. God hadn't left us. God's work was worth remembering. We were still here. And if we were still here, then we were worth spending time talking about, and listening to, and repeating over and over again in hopes that things would change, and that we would feel love, and that we would feel hope when hope felt as elusive as liberation. Our bodies were our gospel. Our memories were our weapons.

Maybe that is what makes memory so powerful: It

is the unbreakable cord that binds the pains of the past to the problems of the present and the possibilities of the future. My grandmother, finding a way to be a country Black feminist, through her rough, greasy hands and through her old dark brown eyes, taught me that remembering is not just about remembering what happened to us; it was about remembering the story bound to her body. The kitchen was not just a kitchen. It was not just a home for pots and pans, old grease and white flour, trash cans and a half-working refrigerator. It was a sacred space, a sanctuary of survival, a place where we told our own story. Though she never got to step foot in the pulpit as a preacher in the Pentecostal church, she was, while we were talking and sitting, God's preacher, God's voice. The God she found leaped off old pages of black Bibles into her frail Black body. She found God in the singing. She found God in her cooking; in Sunday morning praise and worship; in dancing; in stillness and in rest; in her grandkids and great-grandkids and her lineage, her testament to survival. This was her witness.

She had a story to tell, something special to say, something to say with her mouth and with her body and with her hands and with her eyes. What I heard that day calling back to me: a revelation that would keep me going in the midst of such chaos. Greasy hands. Frail bodies. Happy hearts. Unsweet Tea. Unsalted chicken. Imagination. Dreaming. Memories. Flooding. Engulfing her. Engulfing me. Engulfing us together.

She rarely likes to talk about it, but she remembers.

WEEKS LATER, I DECIDED TO DO A LESSON ON JESUS and what it meant to remember Jesus. By this time, the kids were familiar with my teaching style and knew that I didn't just want to teach them about the Bible, but I wanted to help them find themselves in the Bible just like my grandma found herself and how she taught me to find myself. I wanted them to know that the Bible wasn't a dead book, locked in history, but a living story, one that they were a part of, and could shape, and could see. I had made them write essays about their families and about their memories and about what they learned and what they wanted to change. This day, I wanted to revisit that lesson and tell them all the things that I'd learned and all the things I felt I could change in my own family. The sky was overcast. There was not the familiar breeze or the familiar sun or the familiar smells. As I bounced in between schoolwork and finding a video to play for the beginning of class during our devotional time, I saw her walking in. The frown on her face.

"They killed him, Mr. Stew," she said.

"They shot him," she said in a frantic voice.

"They shot at him twenty times," she said.

"Mr. Stew, how they kill that man like that?" she asked.

"They killed that man in his grandma backyard," she said.

I was sitting on the bench getting ready to teach my lesson that day when one of my students told me about how she felt about the murder of Stephon Clark. She was shook. I was shook when I saw what had happened as I quickly scrolled on Facebook. *Not again,* I thought to myself. *Not again.*

My children and I were getting used to seeing dead Black bodies, being murdered and being blamed. When I saw the reports, I couldn't say a word. I wanted to say something to her that would comfort her. I couldn't bring myself to it. I was too angry. She was angry. She was enraged. I couldn't blame her. I found myself pausing, picking up my book to read and my journal, grabbing my pen and trying to get back to work. I couldn't. I put my journal and my book down. *He was shot at twenty times. At his grandmother's house.*

"How you feeling?" I asked Jay, trying to get her to voice how she felt. "You can be honest."

"Really?" she asked, not too sure if I was ready for her to be *that* honest.

"Yeah."

"Well. I hate this shit really. It's like they can kill us and just get away with it. It's like that they don't even care. Our lives don't even matter," she said. "I just want this place to change, Mr. Stew. I just want better for us."

I was struck by how raw she processed her emotions. I was sad, too, because I knew that she was learning what it meant to be Black the same way that I had. It meant never really being given a childhood. Never really not having to worry about who would be murdered next who looked like you. Never really having to deal with the pain of a verdict not accomplishing the justice it promised. Never really growing up without fears and having to grow up way too soon. She learned what I learned: This country is exhausting. I hated that the words *terror* and *lies* and *struggle* and *rage* would enter her lexicon too early.

In her recent essay "The Trayvon Generation," Elizabeth Alexander paints a picture of the young people growing up in the past twenty-five years. We are a generation that has known that hashtags for us are also history books, chronicling the journey of young people who look just like us.

Their journeys have ended. Too early. Dreams destroyed, as we watched the stories come across our feeds, forcing us once again to call out in helpless rage. "These stories," Alexander writes, "helped instruct young African-Americans about their embodiment and their vulnerability." They were stories of terror. They were stories that didn't keep one's eyes in the skies too long. We knew that we had to come back down and learn how to survive this world. These stories let us know that "anti-black hatred and violence were never far." My classroom, like my grandmother's kitchen, was a sanctuary of survival.

Alexander worries about our generation, a generation of young people who undoubtedly are dealing with depression and trauma, just like our parents, just like my grandmama. Each day my students walked into my classroom they saw this world and they knew that so much is wrong in it. They were angry—but most of all they were numb. It's the type of numb that feels but doesn't, that wonders and dreams but doesn't. They were always looking for ways to numb themselves to this present danger. It's not that life is all about danger, or all of life is about the threat of death; it is not. It is that the threat and danger is real, as real as our breath, as real as our life. It is as real as the rain dripping on your face as a child when you find out how soothing and different the water is. Only thing is, the water, unlike the danger, is not trying to get rid of you. It is not trying to ruin you.

That was a hard time for me as a teacher. I really didn't know what I was doing. I was trying to teach these ten-, eleven-, and twelve-year-olds how to learn history, how to talk about themselves and the past, how to know that history is not dead, and that the memory of our successes and our failures lived in them and in me. I was trying to teach them how to care for the oppressed, how to live like Jesus. I was trying to teach them to make sense of their bodies, where their bodies lived, how their bodies were taught how to love and how to fail and how to grow up. I was trying to teach them how to talk about their country and the ways both the country and the church fails to love and teaches us to fail at love. I was trying to help them and myself unlearn toxic ways we were learning to be human, and Christian, and American. I was trying to teach them how to be alone and how to be together and how to make a difference and how to heal and how to tell a better story than the ones we were offered.

I wanted them to know that any progress that has been made in our country is not because our country has been so good or is always progressing. It is because we have refused to shut up and play, shut up and pray, shut up and work. We have refused to be silent about our pain, our struggle, and our dreams. It is because we have refused to give up faith in ourselves, in God, and in the possibility of justice, liberation, and healing.

Black Lives Matter was not just a rallying cry of protest for Black bodies. It was a love letter, a monument, a testimony, a hallelujah, a yes Lord, a sermon, a dream. It was a cry to remember and love hard, and to love publicly and to love honestly, and to tell the truth, and to be better, for all of us.

I wanted better for Stephon.

I wanted better for them.

I wanted better for me.
I wanted better for us.
I wanted better.

IN HER ESSAY "THE SITE OF MEMORY," TONI MORRISON writes that "the act of imagination is bound up with memory." She remembers how the Mississippi River was straightened to make room for houses, and for livable conditions, and better crops, and a better life. From time to time, the river floods over these places. She stops to examine one word: *flooding.* That is what is happening when the water comes crashing down the red Mississippi clay, filling up barren places, washing away the cracks. "It is remembering," she writes, "remembering where it used to be. All water has a perfect memory and is forever trying to get back to where it was." It was trying to find its way home.

Out of the imagination, Morrison writes, Black people dreamed of a new world. These dreams told a story of hope of those trying to get back to where they were. They dreamed of a day where our souls, the souls of Black folk, could rest. Stories of hope in the midst of despair, stories of rage in the midst of oppression, stories of power in the midst of pain, love in the midst of brutality, this rush of imagination, says Morrison, "is our flooding."

What is the goal? *Witness.*

Our bodies and our beauty and our creativity and

our honesty and our failures and our dreams and our hopes, these all become witness. There is a longing, a searching for a place to stand, a place to be in a country that is hell-bent on us not being. We witness our audacity to survive. We witness young children caught between camera recordings and hot lead. We witness young children wondering if they will be next. We witness mothers crying out behind podiums for their babies' humanity. We witness conversations around kitchen tables. We witness it all. We witness the light. We witness the loss. We witness the lost.

MY PHONE RANG ONE DAY. IT WAS EARLY. "DANTÉ," my mom said with a trembling voice, "your granddaddy got out of the house early in the morning. We don't know where he is. We have been looking for hours now. He's lost." My heart immediately sank to the carpet floor. I felt turning, and twisting, and trembling.

I grabbed the olive oil in the green bottle. I rubbed it in my hands. I put it on my head like Bishop did when we stood in line during service to get prayer. I got on my knees and prayed and prayed and prayed. Whenever we would get in trouble or would get sick, my momma would call for the elders of the church and they would pray for us. It may not have changed our situation, but it did make us less ashy and more greasy and more comforted. So I prayed my oily prayers. The flood that came over my body was violent. It was rushing from my stomach to my neck. My mouth was dry. I started to feel my palms sweat. *How is Grandma doing? What is she thinking about right now? What is she feeling? Is she afraid? What is going on?*

I was terrified. I was angry. I was tired. I needed some air. So I walked outside; the morning was still, quiet. There were clouds covering the sun. I was afraid. So very afraid. So very sick. The cold, brisk air came and it went. My heart was racing, and I hadn't even started running yet. I cried. I cried because I was not around. I cried because I didn't want to lose him. He was lost, and there was nothing I could do about it. I prayed another terrifying prayer. *God. Let him be found alive.*

"What's the update?" I asked my momma when I called. Jas and I were in California. My family was in South Carolina. That distance felt terribly far that day. It felt like ages away and I felt powerless and terrified because there was nothing I could do but just wait on a call. I tried to convince myself that my granddaddy would be alive. But if I'm honest, I had started to prepare myself for his death because I didn't want to have my heart shatter again at the pain of another cold, dead Black body. I could not take the thought of abruptly learning of his death. So I prepared myself. And I prayed. And I tried to remember so much I had experienced of him and had known and had talked about. I wanted him to live, but I was prepared to grieve if he died. "Everybody is still looking," she said. "What's the update now?" I asked her again an hour later. "Everybody is still looking." The next hour. The next hour. The next. I could hear faint voices in the background that had been up for hours.

The night before, they were all at church together. My granddad was lucid; he was himself, talking with everyone. Now, he was lost.

I was angry. I was angry that he was lost. I was angry at how mean this disease was. I thought to God: *Why would you let this happen? Hasn't he been through enough in this godforsaken country? Hasn't he suffered enough?*

My mom called me a few minutes later. "Sister Jones said the Lord told her 'You gonna get your daddy back,'" my momma said. "Go look for him one more time, Deb," Sister Jones instructed her, telling her all these things she said God let her know. My momma resolved to look again. Everybody was tired. She was tired. She was angry. She was sad. They all took a break. Then they got back to it again.

She said she heard in her spirit, "The river, Debra. The river." *Go back to the river.* As children, we could never go to the river. My momma would always warn us about the snakes and the wild hogs and all the ways we could die because we could not swim. The river terrified me as a kid. I had imagined ghost stories of people who didn't listen to their mommas and didn't make it back. I had thought about all the times De-paul would go and take his gun just in case a snake or a hog came. I knew I was fast, but I didn't want to have to run for my life or to my death. They had a search party looking everywhere for my granddaddy. Some took a break. Some drove to the other side of town. Some stayed to comfort my grandmother.

"Y'all," my mom called out to my family members at the house, as they gathered for a snack before heading out again, "let's go back to the river one more time." Everybody was tired but they agreed. The dogs had picked up his scent; they ran through a wooded area as the sun was beginning to set. My family could hear the water as they followed the dogs through the woods. *Go back to the river.* Everybody started calling his name over and over. Rubin! Rubin! Rubin! No answer.

They knew wild coyotes ran through the bushes, old trees, and dark leaves. They knew of the wild hogs, snorting, aggressive. They knew of the water moccasins, poisonous, deadly. Fourteen hours had passed, he was still not found, he had no meds, he had no cover. His frail body, exposed. *Go back to the river, Deb. Go back to the river.*

They walked across the embankment, on the high side, so they wouldn't fall off what my momma and them as kids called *the cliff.* Rubin!

"Hey!" a voice cried out in the distance.

"Be quiet, everybody!" my momma said, motioning everybody to be still, silent.

"Daddy! Rubin!" she cried out.

"Hey!"

"We found him! We found him! We found him!" everybody shouted. They found him sitting underneath a tree by the river. His gray hoodie with the red rooster on it was covered in mud. His frail body was still alive. My momma called me to tell me the news. I shouted out and cried because he was alive. They rushed him to the hospital; he was alert and alive.

"Daddy, can you sing me a song?" my momma asked as he lay in the hospital bed. He started humming, clapping, and singing: *I know prayer changes things. I know prayer changes things. Yes, I know prayer changes things.*

He didn't know where he was at, but he knew he could sing as he lay, his body covered in a white gown with blue dots on it. It washed over him like fresh country rain, steady yet patient, healing.

I visited him when he got home. I walked up again to the old red brick house in Sandy Run, South Carolina. I walked in the door and saw his smiling face. He was laughing. He was laughing. He was singing. He was dancing.

"Granddaddy," I said, as we sat down on the couch days after he had returned home, talking about El Paso, Texas, the place that he barely remembers but always talks about. "You still got your dance moves?" He paused. He rubbed his bald head with the patches of white on the side. He looked at me. He looked me in the eye. "Well . . . I don't know," he said. "But I'm still here."

He may have lost some memory, but still he remains. That is his story, here. That is our story, our Black story. There have been things snatched from us; the nation and its people have stolen from us.

He doesn't remember his time living in El Paso, the miles and miles he walked to school in South Carolina; he doesn't remember every heartache and hallelujah that brought him to where he is today; he doesn't remember all those John Coltrane tunes that he used to play on that old piano. He doesn't remember the songs he used to sing, the old outfits he used to wear, the card games he used to play, the drives we used to take up and down I-95. He doesn't remember the prayers we prayed around the dinner table, the prayers that he led because he was like a pastor to us. He doesn't remember how proud he was of me when I first put on the jersey, or when I got married, or when I had Asa. He doesn't remember traveling all the dusty country roads, picking up kids for practice, driving all those Black folk to the polls when they learned their voices could be heard. He doesn't remember Martin. He doesn't remember Rosa. He doesn't remember the movement or the struggle or the suffering or the terror. And maybe that is okay. Maybe in the loss of memory, he gained his body back in ways this country could not steal from him.

He doesn't remember.

But we do.

When he can't remember, we hold his story. And still he is found.

"Breathing life back into the past, pulling from the ranks of your history," Imani Perry writes, "is how you build yourself. You are born to something and someplace; you become a living accord and road. This is how we move forward." This is how we have remembered. This is how we have survived. This is how we find home again.

This is how we learn to love.

PIECES.

The world is not a pleasant place
to be without
someone to hold and be held by.
—NIKKI GIOVANNI

I worry about my son, Asa, so much.

He's only two years old, but I know deep down the world that I have to prepare him for. I am a husband, I am a father, I am a writer, I do theology, and I am often afraid, very afraid. It is not fear because I don't have the right answers. I have read enough books, I have thought deeply over coffee about theology and the answers to the weight of hatred in this country. I am not afraid because I do not know. I am afraid because I know that one day he will become me and will have to wrestle with the same questions that I do. One day he will realize this country loves your production, but it does not value your body.

But he will have to grow up.

I used to lie about what I felt about this country, the ways that our bodies were broken, how little I knew how to navigate it: If I could just keep running from it, then maybe it would all turn out all right. If there was anything I knew how to do, it was run. And it worked—as a kid, I was pretty fast. I would be the one everybody *wouldn't* want to race. I was also a scared kid. If there was danger that I could spot, I would take off.

I would run,
and run,
and run,
and run.
And I would lie,
and lie,
and lie,
and lie.

Maybe this is why I worry so much for him. I don't want him to have to run. I don't want him to have to lie. I don't want him to escape himself. I don't want him to learn the ways I had to learn and fail the ways I learned to fail. I want him to learn how to heal and how to be honest and how to be tender and how to fix the broken pieces in himself and others. Really, I worry for myself and all who look like us. I know that no matter how much we try and run from it all, it will still be there. We have to face it. We have to face the depressing, even violent reality: We are living in a loveless world. I will have to tell him: *Son, you live in a country that does not know and rarely seems to care about loving you or setting you free or giving you hope or giving you good news that will keep you going.*

At times, I wake up in the middle of the night just to touch him, to lay my hand on him and whisper a little prayer, to say a little verse or line from the Bible over him. I am reminded of all the families who prayed over children who never returned again. I am also reminded of the families who did not pray, and their kids never returned to them. I am reminded that you just never know. Like I learned from my momma, prayer or a word can seem like all we can do. It is not magic; it is the miracle of those who know healing can come through words and phrases and unutterable groans and hands touching your body with the oil from the green bottle.

I recently read Imani Perry's letter to her sons entitled *Breathe.* "There are fingers itching to have a reason to cage or even slaughter you," she writes. "My God, what hate for beauty this world breeds." I know what it is to feel like one is bound in this world, the hatred, the learning how to breathe. I know what it means to be crushed and broken into a million pieces. It is almost Herculean one would say. It shouldn't have to be; it should never be so hard to be human. Blackness is not hard—it is beauty, it is revelation, it is life—but being Black in a country that does not love Blackness nor cares to make it safe is. It has been made hard with brutal clarity and consistency. I didn't always know that, or maybe I didn't want to believe it.

I was like my son, innocent, protected, naive. My mother and my father guided me under the shadow of their wings as I tried to find my way. But I knew that wouldn't last long. I had to learn how to fly on my own. I had to learn how to brave the weather. There were only two choices: take flight or be crushed by the weight of the pressure. Sometimes I feel like I never learned the lesson. Sometimes I feel like we have been forced to fly before we knew how or even wanted to.

My sister recently asked me, "Danté, when did you first know you were Black?" I was taken aback by the question because I had never really thought about it. I mean, I knew I was Black, but she wasn't really asking when I knew I was Black. She was really asking, "When was the first time you knew people saw you as Black?" That's the question that is really being asked when we ask that question. "When did you first find out others saw you as a *nigger*?"

I thought about it. This question took my mind back to elementary school. I faintly remember getting in trouble because one of the young boys was picking on me. Instead of just letting it settle and move on, I decided I was going to take matters into my own hands. During our fourth grade class, he would make odd jokes and move things that sat on my desk. This day was no different. He did it again: more picking, more moving. I got fed up and waited until class got settled. I got out of my desk and walked over to his. Looked at him in the face, grabbed his desk with both hands, and picked it up and slammed it down. I did it again and again and again and again. I knew I was probably going to get suspended for it, but I felt better and I was able to get my anger out.

The teacher escorted me to the principal's office. I hated him. I hated everything about him. He had this ol' southern drawl, his white hair always slick, and he always wore his khaki pants over his stomach. Looking back on it, he reminded me more of a warden in prison than a principal in a school. He never had good things to say or things that would make some of us feel better or make some of us know that the things we wore and the things we said were normal and not punishable.

I remember overhearing him talking to my mom in his office one afternoon, as I waited outside. "Danté has a propensity to get in trouble," he said. Of course I was doing stupid things that kids did—talking in class, passing notes—but we all were. Why'd I get singled out—and from the principal, no less? My mother didn't take that well. "I get mad until this day," she told me. "I get mad until this day." I knew that shattered her heart, to hear that her baby boy, who was a kid like other kids, who made mistakes like other kids made, who prayed like other kids prayed, who was in church all week like other kids, would be, once again, an object of America's racist prophecies. I hate it because I know that she was not the only Black momma who would be mad and I would not be the only Black child who would be said to be inherently a troublemaker.

Was that the first time I felt it?

I felt it when I used to get whuppings as a kid. I got whuppings at school; I got whuppings at home. I remember the bus rides home after getting in trouble doing something dumb. The feelings of anxiety would churn my stomach with feelings of rumbling like old soda and turnip greens. I would get to my grandmother's house and not eat the good not-so-salty chicken and the not-so-sweet tea she had ready for us every time we finished the day. I wonder if she knew? I wonder if she knew how scared I was?

When my momma picked us up, I would say nothing, more silent and more terrified, but I knew, I knew she was angry. I don't think she was angry at me but more so angry at what this world thought of me, what it did to Black bodies that looked like mine, what she knew deep down in her bones and in her soul. She knew that she would rather get to me than let the white world do whatever it wanted to do to me.

She still beat me.

I can remember it to this day. I don't forget those whuppings. We would get home, and I rushed to the bathroom, faking that I had to take a dump. I really did. You know that nervous feeling we all felt. I tried to stay there as long as I could because I knew what was coming. I got done, would go in the room and grab the Vaseline like it was anointing oil. I took it and rubbed it all together, put it on the back of my thighs.

"LORD," I would say.

You know.

I am sorry.

Don't let it hurt too much.

In the name of Jesus.

In the *nammme* of Jesus.

Let this be quick.

Whenever I would get whuppings, I knew my mom didn't want to do it. I could see in her eyes that she was caught between fear and love. She was afraid that she would not simply hurt my tender flesh, but that she would wound my spirit. But she said she did it because she loved me. With each hit, "I" . . . "love" . . . another hit . . . "you." I knew she did. I knew she meant it. She didn't want to hurt me; she really did love me. My body being controlled meant I was being loved. I knew that beatings or prayers or hot sweaty sermons or late-night tarrying services were never going to protect me.

I didn't really get angry at my momma. Her whuppings didn't make us more holy, but they did make us a little more moral in public.

Every day I entered back into this world, so deeply saturated and filled with anti-Blackness, I would never be protected, but I could be loved—even if it was a trying, hard kind of love.

But I knew this lesson would never set us free. It was never intended to. *Is this a lesson my son and children, and other people that look like us, learn early? Is this the lesson we carry with ourselves throughout our lives? Is this the lesson that keeps us weighed down? Is this the lesson that we must be freed from? Love and punishment? Threats and danger? Condemnation and control?*

I'm not sure, but I do know that too often our people—beautiful Black people—have their hopes and dreams snatched from them, shattered into a million shards of unfulfilled promises and unrealized futures. Too often our lives and their value have lived on shaky ground. We have had to live both with the possibility of danger and the remembrance of loss. We have had to remind ourselves and our children that life is beautiful but can become tragic in the name of a cellphone, in the name of fear of your body, in the name of economic common sense, in the name of wrong cars, in the name of so many things that remind you that your body is still not loved in the country it lives in.

In the midst of it all, we would be left to pick up the pieces and be forced to learn, whether we wanted to or not, whether we learned how to or not, to put ourselves back together again.

Always have.

Always will.

PRAY ABOUT IT.

God is in control.

We know all things work for good.

I, too, had this hope at one time. My Black momma gave it to me to protect me. White folk gave it to me to keep me silent. I, too, believed it and preached about it. I, too, went to great lengths to prove it to people who looked like me, thought like me, felt like me. I, too, was a prophet in a strange land trying to get people to hold on to something that would make things feel okay, even if we both knew things might never be okay. Offering hope and meaning is a profoundly human task but it is a profoundly harmful task when it always tells an optimistic story. It is a profoundly Christian task as well. Faith and living can take but a few steps before crumbling if they are not tied to something with some weight to it. As a writer, I was learning how to lose this hope to find a better one. I knew that type of reality-blinding—or, better yet, race-transcending—hope as a familiar mystery that had no revolutionary potential to it.

I learned to imitate white writers and their dishonest ways of talking about our country, our faith, and what material we all needed to somehow survive how terrible their lies were. The more I learned how to grow up, the more both my heart and my hands got weary of imitating their ways of being less terrible. I know neither their words nor their voices could imagine my words and my voice and the voices of the many that I carried in my body, to be words and voices that could be more than their limited ways of understanding us. They spoke to my soul, yes, even spoke to my mind, but they rarely took my body seriously enough to put words out in the world that would free them and us. So I gave it up. I gave up on both of our abilities to give something we never saw: a better faith and a better country.

The more I read James Baldwin, the more I read Toni Morrison, the more I read Richard Wright, Gwendolyn Brooks, Langston Hughes, James Cone, J. Deotis Roberts, Pauli Murray, and even Martin Luther King, Jr., the more I saw them follow the same story.

They were once optimistic. Then they encountered the enduring struggle in this country. Hope was shattered. They had to learn how to pick up the pieces. They made something better. It happened again and again and again. They weren't trying to convince white people that we were more than they said; they were really trying to love us by showing us that we were not crazy. They were in the long line, as Ta-Nehisi Coates writes, of *dream-breakers*. They were drafted into a tradition of asking the greatest questions of faith, meaning, freedom, and democracy. For them, there were no mountaintops anymore, there were no green pastures to run around in, there was only the wilderness, and we had to find a way out of it together. They had to give up the stuff of dreams, break clear of illusions, and carry their old rugged crosses on their Black backs in a world that was hellbent on crucifying them.

I thought that as a Black Christian, my writing and my news must always crescendo on Sunday, with shouts of joy, and with people dancing to praise breaks, and with lemonade and sweet tea, and with disciples running to tell of the story of the return of the One who was murdered. I knew we all needed more than that.

White people destroyed that in me. I gave up on fantasies like that. Listening deeply to the word and the faith of my ancestors taught me a better and more liberating way. I knew that making sense of my Black experience and my Black body and my Black faith in a white country meant taking my experience, my body, my faith, and my country seriously. I knew that calls and cries for Sunday never would get us to Monday when the smell of hot bacon and cheese grits would be engulfed with the heart-wrenching terror of loneliness, an old and familiar story of praise and pain when Black flesh seemed defeated. I knew Black people were not footnotes in white Christians' stories. We didn't want to integrate or be involved in places that denied our full humanity, debated our full reality, and diminished our full creativity. Many wanted to talk about racism but didn't want to deal with white supremacy. Many wanted to talk about injustice but didn't want to deal with anti-Blackness. Many wanted to talk about unity but didn't want to deal with justice. Many wanted to center white comfort and not Black liberation. We needed to learn how to live and to work and to struggle and to be and to love when the gloomy Monday morning comes once again, and all that is here is our hearts, our minds, and our bodies trying to make it another day, trying to sing in a world where we are bound.

Writing had become a place of sanctuary, a place of following Jesus into the wilderness when I felt overwhelmed. It had become a church, a place where I would meet with God and have the voices of the ancestors guiding me, a sort of spiritual and historical connection, rootedness. I didn't need optimism in those moments; I needed people who understood what it meant to try and fail at being Christian, who could walk with me like a child walks with their parents, like the little children in the embrace of Jesus. I needed weight. The old folk would say, "Don't forget where you come from." I didn't. Their books pulled me in, they never let me go. I didn't know whether I was in the tradition, whether I was doing liberation right, letting words become balms of healing and the stuff that makes kingdoms shake.

I just started to refuse to give empty hope to myself or to people who did not see our humanity. I just tried over and over again, every time I got my black coffee and mustered up some Black words on empty white pages. I tried to give us love, love that would keep us grounded through the shaking.

As a writer, I came to the realization that far more important than people liking my work or even resonating with my work or even using my work to shake things up was me liking myself and liking the complexity of life and believing that I had something worth giving that was saturated in maturity and love. The people who I wanted to like my work were far more interested in being loved than they were in me trying to make them like me or me trying to give them hope or me trying to conjure up something fantastical that would keep one foot in front of the other.

We were not looking for hope.

We were looking for love.

MY SON IS NEXT TO ME.

He is asleep, soundly.

I wonder to myself, "What is he dreaming about?" Do children dream at his age? Sometimes he wakes up screaming and crying, like he saw a ghost or a dead man, something that jolted him out of his peace. He is only two but he knows how to be afraid and scream out "Daddy" with a helpless high pitch. I get it—that's what babies do. But it feels too early. *Was it a nightmare? How does he know how to jump and jolt and cry out and scream?*

I have been thinking so much lately about his future and our future together. I hurt to think that some of the nightmares that jolt his body out of sleep at night will jolt his body when he is awake and moving and walking in our country. I have been thinking about how to dream in a time of terror and how not to destroy his innocence. I do not want him to fall victim to the American way of dreaming, its way of believing itself to be innocent while it killed our people and turned their suffering into dreams of a color-blind America. I refuse to teach him that way of dreaming. I also refuse to teach him that dreams will save us. It neither saved us from failure nor saved us from all of the bullets and ballots and messages and policies and all the ways this country failed us. I refuse to teach him that dreams will never end in nightmares, that his palms won't be sweaty, that night won't seem like eternity, and that every wounded soul can be healed. I refuse to teach him to dream that way. But I will teach him how to love, and how to really love by redefining dreaming, and living, and believing in something that seems elusive. I will teach him that dreams don't always uplift; sometimes they destroy. But I dream anyway because I'm not so arrogant to believe that neither we nor others can somehow make it without dreaming. To live, to love, to talk about God's future and resurrection and hope is to dream a little bit. Dreams are not always the stuff of fantasy and failure. It is also the stuff of survival and a deep love of life and one's future.

I think my worrying has somehow turned into dreaming. At least that's what I tell myself. I don't want to worry about him. I want to dream.

I have been thinking about so much more than that. I have been trying to read and to write and to try and leave him with something that would make him proud that his daddy took the bits and pieces of himself and of us and tried to love us whole again. At least he can be consoled and held. That's what our parents have been doing for years. They have been taking what little they had, making it smell good and feel good, and laying it out for us to find some sense of meaning in the madness. That is how they coped.

His father spent too many years drunk on lying his way into feeling safe and free. In the face of a loveless world, maybe he will see our Blackness not as I did—as liability, as embarrassment, as something to be devalued and destroyed—but may he see it as it was intended by our Creator: that our Blackness was not meant to be controlled but cherished, set free, and a force, a Spirit, a movement, a gospel. I think he will get it one day: Blackness is less about survival and endurance and more about belonging, embracing, and loving deeply.

Love is elusive when survival and searches for meaning become your pressing need. But love is probably the only weapon strong enough to keep my legs going when my knees buckle as I hold him close to my chest and imagine a world better than the one we are offered.

Love is not a fixed set of rules; love is not mere truth and consequence. Love is as fierce as it is invisible; as real as it is elusive. My son joins us alongside our stumbling toward love—and how we all learn and still learn how to love well.

He is about to become a big brother.

"We're pregnant," my wife told me. I could see the excitement on her face. "We're having another baby." I was both excited and terrified. A part of my body feels the stiffening anxiety that I remember when she had Asa. I tried not to read all of the bad things that could happen in delivery but I couldn't help but be drawn to the terrifying reality of Black women and the loss of their beautiful children and the loss of their beautiful lives because the system to which their bodies and their children are born and grow up in treats them less than beautiful.

"What do you think we're having?" she asks after an ultrasound appointment.

"I don't know," I respond, turning the black and white images back and forth.

"The face looks like Asa," she says, laughing. Sure enough, as in Asa's sonograms, the baby's hand is nestling to the side of its cheeks.

"I think it's a girl," I tell her.

"Really?"

"Yeah, I think it's a girl."

"Whatever it is, I just want it to be a good and healthy delivery and baby."

I just want it to be safe. For her. For us.

I didn't tell her how terrified I was. I was happy, I was joyful, I felt the flutters like I felt when we first laid eyes on one another, those heart-racing feelings that you know are real but also know will leave. I was so, so afraid.

Recently I have been reading Elizabeth Alexander's collection of essays *The Black Interior* again. She knew that in the interior lives of Black folk, there was always something more than we imagined: "complex black selves, real and enactable black power, rampant and unfetishized black beauty." She knew there was a space that was hidden, sort of like the rooms in Grandma's house that we couldn't go in. She knew that Black life was more beautiful and more terrible than what any of us could imagine. She wonders, with each day's news of violation and violence, "What might we hope for and work toward?"

That question haunts me.

What do I hope for and want to work toward for me, my Black wife, my Black children, our Black bodies, our Black futures?

It haunts me because I know how much I have lied as a writer and how much I have lied to myself and how much I have tried to tell the truth, even when I knew the truth may never really bring the outcome that I desired but could actually reveal parts of me that I never wanted to see or confront or to imagine possible or to dream or to fight. It haunts me because there remains so much protection, so much easy fiction that will need to be broken, to be set on fire, to liberate the truer beauty and terror under-neath. If I want hope for anything real, I must first deal with the fiction.

There were so many times I said triumphantly, "I have hope!" when in reality my knees were buckling and my chest was tight with the weight of both dreams and nightmares. I knew that being a part of this long history of Black folk trying to love us and heal us meant that I had to confront in myself the worst of myself, the terrible.

I had to imagine my body beyond the destruction. I had to imagine myself as holy and beautiful. I had to imagine myself as not being bent and broken under the weight of limited imagination, misguided statis-tics, and never-ending pursuits to find ways to blame us and bruise us. I would be forced to do what my parents did: Give those babies hope even if you don't have it yourself. I would be forced to help them find hope even if I didn't find it myself. "Children have never been good at listening to their elders," James Baldwin writes, "but they have never failed to imitate them."

We were once children and we carried the best of us and the worst of us in our minds and in our spirits and in our bodies. I know that my children will carry the best of us and the worst of us in their minds and in their spirits and in their bodies.

They will carry the weights that we carry and the weights that carried us and the weights that we hated and never wanted on our bent backs as we tried to love and lift one another up. They will carry the fear, the terror, the dread of what it means to carry weights on your body that will crush you if you let them. They will carry the failures that we pass down to one another and that we throw on one another and that we force one another to swallow bitterly because we are human just like everybody else. But they carry so much more. They will carry the faith that has kept us in the storm as our ships were sinking and we held on to one another and to our broken pieces as we imagined our bodies and our spirits resting on shores that our elders' bodies knew and rested upon. They will carry the love, a deep audacious Black love, that sometimes makes you holler and forget that the weight is on your back and on your hands and in your house and all up and down these concrete streets that we are marching. They will carry pieces of us as we carry pieces of them as we all try to find something meaningful, something powerful, something beyond ourselves. They will carry our breaking, our shattering, our picking up, and putting back together again.

That haunts me because I know that the weights they carry are the weights we carry and we just want to lay down our burdens and rest a little bit. We want our memories and our bodies to be handled with care. It haunts me because it is so, so hard to imagine a day, a hope, a fantastic Dream, where the weights are no more.

Where bodies are not broken.

Where bodies are not wounded.

Where the pieces of ourselves are put together again.

Where we are free.

Where we are *home*.

AMERICAN.

In accepting both the chaos of history and the fact of my total end, I was freed to consider how I wished to live—specifically, how do I live free in this black body? It is a profound question because America understands itself as God's handiwork, but the black body is the clearest evidence that America is the work of men.

—TA-NEHISI COATES

One morning late last year, I went for a run. The sun was barely creeping up as my lungs were filled with brisk air. The sweat began glistening my face like baby oil. The faded orange and blue streaks that go across the California skies began to appear. My headphones were in. J. Cole blasted in my ears as I took deep breaths in between each stride.

Too many niggas in cycle of jail . . . We coming from a

long bloodline of trauma / We raised by our mamas, Lord, we gotta heal.

The music played, but I could hardly focus on what he was saying. I was too focused on my breaths. I passed the old cemetery full of old dead bodies. Where they were it was much colder, much darker, much lonelier than where I was.

I kept running. My heart was still racing. My legs started to remind me of how out of shape I was, how bad the burgers that I ate were for me, my body, and my lungs. The longer I ran, the more weight I felt. It got too heavy for me to keep going. I stopped, pulled my phone out of my running pouch, and started to put J. Cole on repeat. The beat, the lyrics, and the melody became a lot clearer as the beat, the lyrics, and the melody became louder than the beat of my heart I could hear in my ears. I began to walk slowly and say my morning prayer. I needed a rest. I queued up an audiobook of the Bible on my phone. Words from the Bible began washing over my spirit like silent hugs.

There was nobody out.

Just me. My sweaty black shirt. My sweaty Black body. My sweaty Black hands as I gripped my hot black phone.

Cracked concrete and houses whose shapes were as foreign to me as the California weather in late fall and as foreign as my body to people who rarely got close enough to bodies like mine. Between the place I was running and the place I had run from is a racial barrier as thick and as enduring and as visible and as normalized as one could imagine. It is the American way: Zip codes determine where bodies can rest and lie and build. I wish that I could say that it was foreign to my mind but I had become hypersensitive to the social order of whiteness. I could see whiteness wherever I went. I had to. I had been taught to be careful and to be watchful and to be prayerful that the ways I saw whiteness and the ways whiteness saw me would be less toxic, less dangerous, and more human.

I learned real early where I'm from not to run too late at night or too early in the morning in places that I didn't know and that didn't know me. The farther I got away from South Carolina, the further I distanced myself from those lessons my parents had tried to teach me. They knew what could happen. They gave me, my brothers, and my sister talks around dinner, and on the way to church, and while we were cleaning up.

When I left, I stuffed my ID in my socks like my wife tells me to every time I leave for a run. "Be careful," she says, as she looks me in my eyes.

I turn away laughing. "I'll be good," I say. "I won't be long."

"Your phone charged?" she asks.

"Of course," I say as I exit.

I wasn't worried about anything, I felt good. I was having my morning time with Jesus. "Even though I walk through the valley of the shadow of death," the well-produced white voice read from my Bible app as I listened to the Psalms, "I will fear no evil."

"I . . . will . . . fear . . . no . . . evil," I told myself. I repeated it. I repeated it again. And again. And again.

I walked a little farther. I looked in the distance, about ten feet in front of me, and there was this white man on his porch. As my eyes went from my phone to the concrete in front of me and back to my phone again, I noticed his white hands holding a black camera. It was still. It was pointed in my direction. He was taking pictures of me.

The longer he held his camera pointed in my direction, its lens set on my sweaty body, not moving, the more I got confused, the more I got scared, the more I got angry. At first I thought he was taking pictures of the old green trees behind me in front of the man-made creek that stood between us and the children's playground. I thought he was trying to catch the streaks running across the California skies as the sun beat across my face like I was. Then I realized his white hands holding his black camera were surveilling my Black body. I felt numb. I could no longer feel the sweat running down my face and down my back. My hands began to tremble.

Questions began to come into my mind. *What do I do? Where do I go? Do I run?* I asked myself. *What if this is the morning?* I asked myself. *What if he kills me?* In that moment, all the fears, and all the warnings, and all the anger, and all the terror that existed between Black people and white people in this country revisited me. In that moment, my body was shook, and I didn't know if I would make it home. I don't think I know how to describe what that felt like. I don't know if there are words that can describe what it means to be shot with memories I've only seen on TV screens in documentaries and read in books and heard from my mother's lips as I was told to be careful in foreign parts that I didn't know and that didn't know me.

"It's a good morning out here, isn't it?" I said.

He didn't answer.

My heartbeat started to pick up again.

"It's a good morning?" I said once again.

He didn't answer. My palms got sweaty again.

He was not looking for lush images of sunrises and empty parks children played on and cracked concrete and green trees and sidewalks with dusty benches. He was looking for evidence. My sweaty, lean, Black, and tired body became evidence.

"Why are you photographing me?" I asked.

He said I didn't belong there.

"You said you don't think I belong here?"

"Correct." He says nothing else.

"Why don't you think I belong here?" I asked, as if me being respectful to him was going to shield me in this situation or get him to finally see me as a human or finally make me feel better as I endured the audacious ways white people in this country have harmed Black people like me. It did not. It could not.

"I'm not arguing with you," he said as he walked back into his house.

I felt powerless.

I felt terrified.

My body was wet.

My body was hot.

My body was numb.

I was full of rage.

I was full of terror.

I couldn't even call the cops because they might have mistaken me for the aggressor.

No matter how upstanding a citizen, how moral a man, how Christian a preacher, how good of a family man, how anything I was—in one swift motion, this man had emptied me of power. I'm sure he didn't even think twice; I'm sure he forgot about the moment seconds after it happened.

But would he forget it if he had felt what I felt? The humiliation and terror coursed through my body and turned into something else.

Rage burned up my body. I wanted to force him to see my humanity. Wanted to grab him by the neck, drag him out of his house, and shake him awake. I wanted him to feel my pain, my humiliation, and what it was like for someone to believe themselves to rightfully have power over your body, and to put you on the ground, and to suffocate you in the worst ways possible.

To watch his eyes well up with tears and go blood-shot red and to feel like you can't do anything to save yourself. That thought took over my body. It was the first time I wanted to kill a man. Years of untamed rage, of humiliation, bubbled up to the surface in that moment, of white people never really caring about how much they had killed us and forced us to watch our babies and our mothers and our fathers be killed in ways that should never have been possible. I wanted to ruin him like he had ruined me and how his people had ruined us and how the country that we all were living in put up with their ruining. I wanted to be like a white man and live to tell the story.

I wanted to believe that violence would redeem my body. I wanted to believe that I could be terrible and get away with it and get rewarded because of it and be protected by it.

I guess I had learned how to be American.

How do we live in a country and with people that claim your faith but make claims on your body?

How do we live in a country that believes itself to be exceptional?

How do we live in a country that does not believe you to be worthy of loving and surviving and being free?

How do we live in a country where millions believe you should have stayed enslaved?

How do we live in a country that clings to myths that are killing us, that says it loves you while betraying you? What does it mean to be caught between truth and myth? What does it mean to love it and live in it and believe in it and pray for it and preach in it and not be killed by it?

And how the *hell* do we love?

A few weeks after that morning, the verdict for the murder of Botham Jean came down. He, a year ago, had become another hashtag declaring the carelessness this country has toward Black bodies, our beautiful children being held in our memories and not in our arms. My soul was filled with grief as I thought about what that man did to me, what he said to me, and the ways we all have normalized Black suffering. I wanted him to feel as bad as I felt, I wanted others to see how terrible he had been, how painful it is to stare at your beautiful Black face, your dark brown eyes, your curly hair, and have to tell yourself how beautiful your Black face, your dark brown eyes, and your curly hair actually are. It is a condition that no human being should have to face. It is a condition that millions of Americans have chosen for this country. It is a story as old and as painful and as enduring as the country we live in. No amount of Bible verses, no amount of hot sweaty sermons, no amount of hymns on twisted lips, no amount of long midnight prayers can protect you from the suffering, the exhausting weight of crucifixion, with seemingly no hope of the bright Sunday morning. It may not protect us, but it does let us know we do not endure the suffering alone in the dark. It lets us put our feet back on the ground, straighten up our backs, and refuse to allow white people to have the final story on our bodies, on our children, on our sacred spaces in warm living rooms, early morning drives to work, and the laying on of hands as our children go to sleep, as each of us wake up once again to the shattering.

My wife and I sat on the couch as I scrolled through Twitter. Then a video appeared of Botham Jean singing a William Murphy song. There was no music. No loud drums or the reverberating sound of pianos and organs. There were just him, his Black body, his strong Black voice, and a full room of Black folk singing praises to a God who understood how hard it was to sing praise and to not be crushed under the weights. His hand motions the crowd. He sings. His is a sound of assurance, a sound of possibility, a sound of trusting that your tomorrows will be able to be endured. They were so joyful. So, so joyful. He was one of theirs, he was precious, he was talked about by his family and friends. And now, he is but a memory, his voice only to be heard, not felt, not touched, not alive. He is dead.

Amber Guyger stole it all from him. She and the white man on the porch believed the same thing about us that we tried not to believe about ourselves: *You must suffer and be killed, never to rise again.*

Many in our religion have identified suffering with devotion, making it a sort of magical feat of human achievement to withstand the weight of the worst life has to offer. For us, us Black folk, I don't think we have ever believed that. We have never believed that we must suffer in order to have God love us. We have never believed that Jesus looks upon our country's insatiable desire for our suffering with a smile. We did not, we do not, but Amber Guyger and the white man did. They believed our suffering to be natural, final, spiritual, moral. They have grown up in a country with the rhetoric of racism and white supremacy and white innocence. They have heard it and they have believed it. They believed it and they acted on it. They acted out a history that they have known and that has known them.

We have not believed like they have. We have believed we should survive and, more than survive, we must be human, we must be free, we must be American in the most beautiful ways possible.

Since then I have tried to find ways in my reading

and in my writing and in my preaching and in my prayers to think deeply about these questions, the ways it haunts my weary soul, the ways it forces me to face things that I'm afraid I don't have answers to. I have tried to find ways to understand a place that has yet to understand itself. How do you live as a free Black body, a free Christian body, a free young body?

A part of me wants to love our country so hard, so deeply, so vastly. Yet a part of me feels so foreign, so unfamiliar, so angry, so exhausted that I live in a place that has had a profound commitment to deny those who look like me the blessings of the Dream. America, our country, has neither known us nor the God it proclaims to love and serve. Ta-Nehisi is right: *This country, this beautiful and terrible place of our birth and suffering, is the work of men.*

I don't know if I have the answer to any of those questions. I believe they are worth asking and I believe that one day we will all have answers. As the old folks would say, we will understand it better by and by. But more than any answers I could conjure up, I must give myself and others something that will make us shout in the fire. Making sense of what it means to be Black in this country and the ways that we have been Black and learned how to not be destroyed and the ways that we have been Christian and held on to Jesus and held on to ourselves and actually loved and imagined a new day for our faith and our country that has often given us neither love nor hope. These are the things unseen that must be learned and cherished and protected at all cost.

I RECALL SINGING A SONG AS A CHILD IN ELEMENTARY school, in the old beat-up trailers that teachers taught in and that we students learned in. It was the song "Proud to Be an American."

We are taught to cherish the best things of America: American art, American beauty, American life, American games, American words, and old dusty American documents, and to be proud of the ways Americans did not fail. We are taught to be American in the same way. We are taught that we belong here and that others belong here and that we are all equal and that what happened in the past is over. We are taught that our history is a story of triumph, the great American spirit, and that tragedy never comes from us or is never brought about by those who say they serve us. We are taught that there is nothing wrong with this country; we are taught America always makes the best decisions and is never to be criticized. It is a powerful myth.

Our myths give the American imagination its oxygen. We breathe toxic air. Our myths give us cover. Our myths allow us to believe that the words *progress* and *equality* and *honest* and *love* are as American as you know yourself to be. We learn to call home the place of our pleasure and our pain, a place of destiny and deliverance. Pastors and politicians and people imagine the country to be Christian and therefore blessed by God and never in the wrong and worthy of devotion. They believe the country is the kingdom of God when all things point to it being an empire that dares not face the prophets. They believe there was a time when the supposed greatness of this country included those who look like me. It did not, and even until this day, it has been a mighty, mighty struggle to believe that those who look like us are those who made America what it is and what it can become. Our bodies are simply the clearest evidence that this country is the work of men; many have used our bodies to speak of the exceptional possibility of America.

Our symbols tell a story of us that we often dare not face. The symbol of the flag and the cross tell us that this country is Christian and loving and just and therefore right in all it does. Hands are laid on Bibles and verses are plastered across symbols of American pleasure and power, giving them the divine blessing of protection and progress. There is another symbol powerfully at work here: *the Black body.* The symbol of the Black body in White Houses and in white schools and on white fields and in white rooms and in white families and in white churches tells us of the exceptional nature of white people in this country to give up their destruction and be saved and be delivered. Barack Obama represented for many in this country the idea that we all were beyond race and beyond white supremacy and beyond Black exhaustion. It was a moment of exhalation. Black people had made it. America had recovered from its white supremacist origins. We the people of America were the exception.

We went asleep in the dream of exception and woke up to the nightmare of anti-Blackness. The symbol of free Black bodies awakened us to the exceptional ways this country and the people of this country learned how to betray its possibilities. Anti-Black racism was not the exception; it was the norm.

If there is anything exceptional about our country, it is the exceptional ways we have avoided being honest with ourselves. It is the exceptional way that our country has taught us to lie to ourselves and one another. It is the exceptional ways that our country has told us that the white supremacist capitalist patriarchy is God's given. It is the exceptional ways the country has failed at loving us and reforming itself. It is the exceptional ways we have justified, evaded, and even denied our violence. It is the exceptional way that America has betrayed justice and progress on the altar of white fear and white comfort. It is the exceptional way the country has identified with Jesus while ironically crucifying those whom Jesus would stand with and linking arms with those whom Jesus would stand against. It is the exceptional way that we have loved a country and people who have not loved either the country or us in ways that are honest and worth saluting.

To be American is to learn real early that the best stories must be told about ourselves and our country, to believe that the worst of those alive would never be grown out of this soil. "That would never happen here," some say. We are well fashioned in the coziness of lies. Here in America, we learn that to be American is to be terrible, terrible to yourself, terrible to people who look like you, terrible to people who you have been led to believe were taking what was rightfully yours, terrible to the ground that gives you breath, terrible to the many beautiful humans who have known how terrible we have been and how terrible we can become.

How could we, so caught up in our terrible ways of being together, ever imagine something more beautiful, more loving, more honest? That, too, is American. We've learned to kill dreams and dreamers and to avoid our darkness and nightmares and to conjure up prayers and protest and power and possibility in a place that hardly even knows us, itself, and how any of us can be free of the lies that damn us.

Maybe that's the America Langston Hughes wanted again, as he wrote "Let America Be America Again." He wanted an America that is more honest, and more free, and less violent, and less racist, and more just, and more loving, and less greedy, and less harmful. He wanted an America that didn't force Black people to write poems just to be heard. He wanted an America that didn't destroy Black people. He wanted an America that was free of white supremacy. He wanted an America that did not believe it had to control the world. He wanted an America where all people could feel safe, secure, and protected.

To give up on the lies and try to make something out of a place confused about you and itself. To love one another enough to create a world where our fellow neighbors are healed, are free, are not alone, are not forced to endure the terrible ways we have learned to live with one another. To know that the things we lost and yearn for just may not come back, or if they do, they may just look unfamiliar, and they may just never be the same, and that will have to be okay. To be able to let go and be able to move on and be able to not be irresponsible and not crush memories and not crush people and learn how to remember and learn how to be complete and learn how to be better. To witness by shaking the foundations of a country in contradiction and imagine a world and imagine ourselves dreaming again. To be better for ourselves and our children.

Better than our *lies.*

Better than our *hatred.*

Better than our *carelessness.*

Better than our *forgetfulness.*

Better than our *failure*.

Being terrible is not the only way of being American.

THERE IS A FORTUNATE THING, IF ONE CAN EVEN CALL IT that, about growing up in a country that has sought to both destroy and dignify you: It allows you a certain perception of its abilities and how afraid it is to face its failures. Many of us have not had the privilege of believing that America and the people of America could love us in ways that did not depend on our exploitation and our assimilation and our silence.

When our ancestors sang about a strange land, they were neither overly religious nor blindly docile. They sang about what they knew deep down in their flesh and in their bones and in their bodies as their flesh and their bones and their bodies endured the worst a country had to offer. There was a sort of folk wisdom in the honest sermons we heard and the lessons our teachers tried to teach us and the stories we hold from big brothers and cousins about how dark it looks, as Derrick Bell writes, at the bottom of the well. We were not and did not intend to be at the bottom because of ourselves. We were because so many in our country believed us to be less moral, less human, more sexual, more violent, and more submissive. We have never forgotten the years that we came up through weights and chains and bars and bullets and badges and ballots that were committed to both our enslavement and our destruction.

People like to say, "This is not the America I know." We heard it about slavery, Jim Crow, civil rights, the nineties, the white backlash to Obama, the brutal murders of children, women, and men in the Black Lives Matter era, and even about the white rage in support of Trump. For years, we have heard that racism, white hostility, white supremacy, and anti-Blackness were white economic anxiety and evangelical displeasure. We've heard it before. And you know what? Those people are exactly right. The shield of whiteness has protected many from the devastating experience of a country we knew the whole time—one in which white lives and white communities and white pain matter much more than ours. It is white supremacy and a profound commitment to white Christian male rule over the world. It is an old, familiar, and enduring story.

It is a story we have died and lived to resurrect something better, more true, more beautiful.

When people say that white bodies in White Houses and white bodies with badges and bullets and white bodies on porches and white bodies with gavels are an accident or an aberration of the American ideal of goodness, they fail to realize that both are as American as we can imagine. There are no accidents. No. They believe themselves to be what *American* fundamentally means.

The hope we have, especially as Black people, is that we will not give up on loving ourselves and a country and a people who have long tried to appease us with performative acts of solidarity while also upholding a system that devalues, disrespects, and oppresses us. That's how whiteness works, and we have long understood that whiteness and white supremacy can't have the last say. We can use and have used every mechanism of resistance so that we can achieve what this country never believed about itself.

I guess now I understand what Maya Angelou and Paul Laurence Dunbar were trying to get at when they used birds to teach a lesson. I guess I understand why we are still here in the midst of the suffering.

One bird was free; the other bird was bound. One is trapped, only able to see freedom in the distance; the other is free, flying in a world that works in its favor. In its weakness, the caged bird opens up his throat still. It gathers courage, strength, power, the will. The bird must sing in a world that has him bound. He must open up his throat, flap his tender and broken wings, and gather itself to travel far beyond the cage, the rough terrain, the terrible pain of its losses.

It is not a happy situation. It does not feel good but it must fly, it must be free, it must travel to a better land, a better home, a better country. It has to learn how to love itself and live in ways different from how others have learned to create a world that does not care about its freedom or survival. That, too, is what we must learn. We must learn to become much more than much of the world holds out for us.

Toni Morrison was right: You wanna fly, you got to give up the shit that weighs you down.

You must give up the weight. You must be free.

BREATH.

Come to me, all you that are weary and are
carrying heavy burdens, and I will give you
rest.
—MATTHEW 11:28

We gon' be alright
Do you hear me, do you feel me? We gon'
    be alright.
—KENDRICK LAMAR, "ALRIGHT"

My friend TB and I were both exhausted. We
were now a bit older, more overweight than
we were in college, but we were back on
the green grass with the white paint marking the
places on the field. Back at Clemson, he was a
quarterback. I was a defensive back.

It was easy to keep in touch with TB after college.
He would always ask about Jas and how she was doing
in the military. I would ask how business was doing,

what he was reading, if he was staying in shape. We both knew so much of our ability to do meaningful things in life meant taking care of both our bodies and our families. So we stayed joking and checking in and reminiscing over old memories, talking about all the ways we used to make the people proud where we came from.

On this green grass and between these white lines, culminating at the orange tiger paw in the middle of the field glistening with orange paint, our Black bodies heard the sound of thousands of people being American: yelling their hearts out for Black boys in South Carolina to win in ways that made these Americans feel like somebody, even if those who won were less than what these Americans wanted to acknowledge. Instead of the exhilarated feeling of our hearts settling down after the clock reaches zero and our bodies are surrounded by Americans who just want to touch the hem of our jerseys and the feeling of being precious, that feeling of having a power so dear as to make Americans jump over concrete brick barriers, we were both fatigued.

We took a rest break at a coffee shop nearby.

"Man, this shit is exhausting," TB said, his voice an uneasy tremble.

I paused. I took another sip of my hot coffee.

"Man," I said, as I tried to find words that would pass the rock I felt in my throat, and the weight I felt in my stomach as my mind replayed over and over the video of the suffering. "It is, bro. It is."

"When this country gonna love us?" he asked.

"I don't know, bro," I said.

We were hanging out that day because we both knew what the other had seen. What we all had seen. He was not looking for answers. We knew neither of us nor this country had answers to why someone like us would have the breath leave his body as millions of people would endure those fleeting moments with him.

We were both Christian, but neither of us had a prayer nor a word to offer one another. We just sat there, our coffees and Bibles cracked open, sitting side by side on the table between us. I remember myself trying to conjure up something that would make us feel better, something that would calm our spirits in ways that seemed soft and familiar. I wanted to tell him so bad that things were going to be okay, that somehow the suffering that we had known and had seen come across our screens was somehow a nightmare that we would all wake up from if we shook ourselves enough. I wanted so much for us both in that moment that we neither had nor could have imagined.

I wanted our bodies to forget the tension. To breathe easy. But the video. The horror. The terror. The trembling in our souls. It held on to us as tight as their hands around our necks, as heavy as Derek Chauvin's knee on George Floyd's.

I WILL NEVER FORGET WHAT I FELT WHEN I SAW George. After the video went viral, a picture of him, from chest up, made its way around social media. I couldn't stop staring at the picture. I was so sad, but I wanted to honor him as best I could. In his face, I saw familiar eyes. I saw my older brother. George's dark face and dark brown eyes reminded me of older cousins. It was a selfie. I had wondered: Where was he? What was he thinking? Did he just leave the store, grabbing a Coke and scratch-off? Did he just leave his family and laugh around the card table? Was he listening to Tupac like my brother did, reciting old verses reminding him of old times? I had wondered all these things. I couldn't answer any of them. The only space between us is an image and a video and a hashtag and a family shattered under the violence of American hatred.

I saw in him neither a saint nor a criminal. I saw in him neither celebrity nor failure. I saw in him neither struggle nor redemption. I saw George. My eyes were beholding a human. A beloved and beautiful Black body.

He is now dead.

He cried for his momma as we watched him die.

He cried for himself as we watched him die.

He cried for us as we watched him die.

He cried and he cried as Derek Chauvin kept his foot on his neck for eight minutes and forty-six seconds.

And the part that hurt the most: None of us could do anything about it.

As the helpless voices cried with George in the background, as they wept as their eyes beheld his controlled body, his breathless body, the same violence that murdered him sent a message to all of us— that Black bodies didn't deserve to be free, cherished, loved, released. Each second screamed at us loudly and violently: *Nigger, you will not live.*

BOTH TB AND I KNEW SURVIVAL WELL. AND THE WAYS our Black mommas and Black daddies and all the Black folk between Black churches and Black neighborhoods tried to love us. And none of it, neither the power of the Blood nor the gun, could protect us. But still they'd try. They tried to conjure up what little they had to try to remind us of something that this America tried to strangle out of us: *Black body, you must survive.*

They prayed and they watched as some of us, like George, like Ahmaud, like Breonna, like Trayvon, like Mike, like Sandra, like all these precious souls, slipped off into eternity. And some of us into oblivion, as we tried to shake ourselves loose of surviving, hoping to escape both our bodies and what these bodies meant to us and our country, to escape into being normal and human and as far away as possible from the darkness. And some of us into resurrection, taking on magnolia-colored wings, flying with the dim lights at our backs like the evening sun, their smiles breaking into weakness as their hearts melted, as another one of us "made it."

Is this normal?

Should human beings be subjected to life being such a vapor, such a game, such a risk as to be alive in a convenience store one moment, to be alive laughing with friends, to be alive driving your car, to be alive playing with toys, to be alive, and to be free, and in the next moment be dead?

I often think about how quickly things in this life can change, how quickly the warmth of flesh could turn to cold hands, and eyes with no movement, and chests with no rising, and hearts that are shattered in a million pieces. I understand what white supremacy has done and will do to us: It will kill us. Slowly. Violently. Publicly. It is a sturdy American wall. Isabel Wilkerson likened this country to an old house. "When you live in an old house, you may not want to go into the basement after a storm to see what the rains have wrought," she writes. "Choose not to look, however, at your own peril." Ignorance is not protection against the rot—it gives the rot its power and longevity. The rot forces us into resilience. It is not normal. No people should be forced.

IN THE WEEKS FOLLOWING THE MURDER OF GEORGE, I saw millions of people across the globe cry out publicly that they didn't want Black people to be forced anymore. They didn't want us to be suffocated under the crushing weight of white supremacy. I saw scores of young folk, fists held high in the sky, their lungs exhausted from all the screaming they did. I saw scores of old folk, some with canes, some in wheelchairs pushed by another, their lungs exhausted from all the screaming they did. I saw scores of gay folk and straight folk, Muslim folk and Christian folk, American folk and global folk, rich folk and poor folk, all lungs exhausted from all the screaming they did. Then I wondered if this was a perpetual state of our human being. Exhaustion. I saw creation, all of creation groaning in the Fire. Signs were held high reading like sermons on Sunday morning, dirt marks kissed kneecaps as many kneeled as in prayer. Americans called to protect Americans were now beating, and spraying, and tossing, and turning, and harming the Americans they so claimed to love. Exhaustion.

As I scrolled through photos from the summer's protests, my eyes beheld a baby girl on my computer screen. A beautiful Black baby girl. Her piercing eyes full of fear, full of rage, full of love, full of exhaustion. Her mask sat at her chin as she screamed from her belly: *No justice! No peace! No justice! No peace!* Her hands are balled. She walks and she walks and she screams for herself and her future. Her hands wave back and forth and she screams again. She has learned what we have learned. She has learned that her precious body is in danger and so she must scream, she must cry, she must march.

At that moment, I had become sad. I had become sad because I knew that no child should have to use her lungs to scream to live and for those who look like her to breathe. I had become sad because it was a familiar story. I had become sad because I wanted to see her run and dance and play and grow up and get old and find love and find faith and find hope. I had become sad because I knew that she would never forget that moment, she would never forget that name. I had become sad because I knew that she, like me, and like all of the folk that came before us, was in search of a better land, a land flowing with milk and honey.

Then I remembered, that was the hope, her Black body, caught between danger and deliverance. She chose to fight for herself, she chose to fight for her people, she chose to scream and to shout and to march and to dance and to throw her hands up and to preach good news and to remember and to shake foundations and rock souls straight, and conjure up ancestral tongues, and hot sweaty sermons, and dark memories, and dear pledges of love, and broken dreams, and bent bodies, and epistles of love, and responsible love. She chose to stand in the face of danger, to hold on to some imagination of a better world, to hope in the midst of social suffering. She chose to keep our memory alive. She became good news for us. It was no creed, no phrase, but love, the love of God at work in one small body. She did not forget. She loved us. She loved us hard.

It is terrible that she has to love us this way. It is terrible that my children and our children have to love us this way. But if they had not loved us and we had not loved them, none of us would have survived.

I looked again at the video and the videos of millions marching in solidarity, and I saw so much more. I saw joy. I saw intimacy. I saw bodies let loose. I saw tears of strength in the face of danger. I saw heaven smiling as love was cast on Earth's threshing floor. I saw so much joy. It was not simply resistance; it was power. I saw the good news. I saw a better story than the story we were offered. The beauty of this moment showed that suffering is not the total image. This is a moment of faith, flying one would say. I see an unexpected glimpse into public bravery, the willingness to rise again. There is something about these images that calls out to me to sit still; to ponder, to anticipate life beyond brutality.

This joy is love dancing with reality, humanity. I

saw the complex and complicated relationship with hope, a tragic but necessary one if it is to become what it can become—beautiful. I saw the place of rest, a place that is able to hold our rage, our hopes, our failures, our dreams, our bodies when they are broken, our hearts when they are shattered, our prayers when they are imagined, our futures that we have not seen yet.

When I saw these images, I saw myself. I saw all the painful memories and tears I cried that I wanted to be released from. I saw all the ways I had been hurt and all the ways I had suffered and all the ways I had failed. I saw all the ways I wanted better for us. I smelled the old metal mics and the old leather. I saw the back roads and the conversations and the laughing and the shouting and the shaking like something got a hold of us. I saw Black boys on white fields, smiles shining like noonday. I saw late-night prayer meetings, rough hands glistening with oil anointing our bodies and our futures. I saw our streets marked with the streaks of our royalty, crowned with glory and honor. I saw bodies back straight again. I saw the dreams that carried us. I saw prayers for mercy, and pleas for help. I saw us being held like newborn babies, caressed and embraced like they believed we were precious.

I saw big cousins and friends, playing cards, drinking liquor, laughing. I saw cops in silver cars reading TO PROTECT AND TO SERVE driving slowly through our neighborhoods, asking questions, rarely smiling. I saw broke-down cars on cinder blocks, and dirt fields with deflated balls, and trailers with spray paint, and old red brick houses with Bible verses meeting you at the door. I saw us running in the woods with broken sticks, family around the dinner table with broken hearts. I saw smiles that are locked shut, buried beneath cold hard dirt, and buried beneath cold dark cells, and buried beneath cold dark hearts and dark hands that harmed them. I saw trees that gave us berries and beatings. I saw streets that gave us blessings and bruises. I saw tears and unanswered prayers and hallelujahs as some slipped off into eternity and some of us slipped into oblivion and some of us slipped up and walked across stages thought impossible. I saw grateful hands clenching their chests, bent bodies, trembling legs. I looked and I saw us, country folk, living and making something of what we had. I look back in wonder at how we made it over. I look back and some of us are gone, and some of us are still here, and some of us are still standing.

And I feel loved. I feel so, so loved.

I cried. I cried because I knew that was the meaning: The hope was in the struggle, God was in the hope, and these bodies will not always suffer. These bodies will not always tremble. These bodies will live. I saw these beautiful Black bodies.

I saw lies.

I saw failure.

I saw terror.

I saw rage.

I saw wounds.

I saw love.

I saw yearning.

I saw country roads.

I saw beat-up cars.

I saw floods.

I saw pieces.

I saw dreaming.

I saw America.

I saw us.

All of us.

We are alive, we are breathing, we are here. We catch our breath. We are exhausted, but we catch our breath again.

ACKNOWLEDGMENTS

Writing this book was as freeing as it was fear-inducing. I wanted to write this book. I wanted to write something that was honest and loving and tender and rigorous and responsible. I knew that I couldn't write this book alone. I was *alone* so many times when I went to put words to pages, and it was a familiar loneliness where magic and ministry happen. It was what while growing up we would call *the midnight hour*. Though metaphoric, it best describes the process of trying to find ways to love in the midst of darkness, trying to find faith in the midst of confusion, trying to bear witness in the midst of terror, trying to find words in the midst of rage—and to do it all without giving up on what I know can be true of all of us. I wrote a book because this book needed to be written and needed a witness, and I believe I did my best to witness to the light within me. This one, first and foremost, was for me and for me in ways I can't even describe on the page. I knew I had to wrestle, and I knew victory wasn't promised. A gift.

Jasamine, my dear wife, you saw this before I ever knew it could be a possibility. You kept me going in ways that can only be expressed by saying, simply, I love you. Whatever I am and whoever I imagine myself to be is but the outward expression of the many ways you have loved me and shown me the way to embrace, and grow up, and get better. Before there were any words in public, there were so many words in private that showed me the light and hope and truth. We done been through it. We been through so much more that couldn't and shouldn't make it on the page. It is for us to know and to witness and to remember and to hold on to. I have cried a lot as I thought about the long nights and hard pages and words that you prayed over me and the ways you gave me space to write and to think. It all mattered then and it all matters now. Thank you, baby. Thank you for believing in me and keeping my eyes on the prize.

To my beautiful children, Asa and Ava. I have thought so much about you as I wrote this book. I knew that I had to write a sort of love letter or an epistle to you so that one day you can look back on this moment and be proud that your daddy found a way to not be destroyed. I don't expect you to follow the way I've gone or make the same mistakes I've made, but I do know that on the way you would have learned how to love God, yourself, your beauty, your wounds, your failures, your quirks, your dreams, and all the things that make you lovely. You would have learned how to make sense of things, or at least try to. You would have learned the meaning of solidarity and faith and all the ways we describe ourselves as better than we are in these present moments. I hope you feel my love as I have felt your future with every page.

Debra Stewart and Calvin Stewart and Depaul Stewart and Dion Stewart and Dominique Stewart, my family, I want to thank you. We have learned so much together over these years. You have taught me so much. We have held both joy and sorrow together in sacred and sad places. We have had ups and downs. We've prayed together and fought together. We're family. Nothing that I am today is without your support, your love, or the many ways each of you hold us together. I hope that you are proud of these words and feel loved and seen and honored when you read them.

To my friends, my day-ones, the ones who hold me down: I'm not sure that I would have made it without each of your being on my team. Really, I'm glad to be on your team. Now just like church, this ain't in no particular order. You know I love each of you with a love that ain't letting go or letting up: Rich V., Josh, Cam, Martin, Ced, Modi, Nef, Chris, Byrd, Hayes, Andrew W., Michael G., Dee (my barber), Tajh, PG, Zebra, Trey, Mary-Anne, Lashana, Michael W., Jemar, Jonathan W. Hartgrove, J. Hill, Derwin, Jason C., Daniel G., Latasha, Lee J., Cole Arthur Riley, Karen P., Matt A., Heath C., Mark Chironna, Tyler B., Katherine S., John O., Ben Higgi, Annie D., Caleb G., Amar P., Dwayne, D. Rob, Gideon, Drew, Andrew Roth, Rashard H., Andre G., Shawn and Alexis, Rasheena D., Leonce, Curtis M., Wanda R., MY WHOLE CANDLER SQUAD, Sarah, Mike M., Andre H., Megan, Fraendy, Major, Jared, Khristi, LA, Maya, Brandy and Lamar, Thea and Jeremy, Jared and Taylor, Darien, Danielle C., Mikaela, Jakeem, Dominic B., Coty, Dom, Cobee, Trav B., and so many more people. If I forgot your name, I ran out of room. You know the love is real though. You all believed in me and loved me and read all these words I gave you as I struggled through this.

To Kiese Laymon, Eddie Glaude, Robert Jones, Jr., Kristin Du Mez, Jason Reynolds, Krista Tippett, Viet Thanh Nguyen, Robert P. Jones, Anthea Butler, Dave Zirin, Peniel Joseph, and Jacqui Lewis: Thank you for your investment in my life and my writing. Real talk, I can't even describe what it means to be young and a writer and to have people like you believe in me and the words I've put out into the world. Each of you actually made me feel like I had something to say, and each of you, in your own way, was inspiration along the journey. Deep thanks.

My editor, Ashley Hong: You truly believed in this project and you really made me a better writer by the time we got finished. You challenged me and pushed me in ways I never imagined. You were a friend to me in this whole journey. I couldn't have asked for better. Your care and tenderness with my words, your way of making me revisit places and pull out deeper beauty and meaning is a gift.

My agent and team, Alex Field and the Bindery, thank you. I remember the first time we talked and how much you believed in me even when I didn't see it in myself. You saw the light. You saw the witness and I am better because of it. You have been a real advocate and have shown up for me in ways one dreams of. I count it an honor to be on the same team.

To my publisher, Convergent, I am grateful that you took a chance and dreamed a little bit. You all remember that, right: Let's dream a little. I think we did that and believe this will help others dream as well.

To the memory and love of all whom we have lost, all whom we still hold on to, and to all we dream can be possible for each of us, I honor you. May your memory, your life, and your love be a blessing, a movement, a change, and a witness.

Lastly, to James Baldwin. I wish you could read

these words. I wish you could see how much of your work I read on this journey. I know I did my best to honor you and your work. I know I did my best to give voice to something deeper and lasting. One day, I'll tell you all about it. Until then, it's praise breaks and prophetic lines: We shoutin' in the fire.

ABOUT THE AUTHOR

DANTÉ STEWART is a speaker and a writer whose work in the areas of race, religion, and politics has been featured on CNN and in *The Washington Post, Christianity Today, Sojourners, The Witness: A Black Christian Collective, Comment,* and elsewhere. He received his BA in sociology from Clemson University and is currently studying at the Candler School of Theology at Emory University in Atlanta, Georgia.